How to make your own
moccasins

Sylvia Grainger

J. B. LIPPINCOTT COMPANY/PHILADELPHIA AND NEW YORK

This book is dedicated to my grandparents,

Grace M. Redman and Ralph W. Redman

Thanks to Lone Bear of East Orange, New Jersey, Alice Kinzel, Louise Mc-Donald, Shirley A. Trahan, and Doug Allard for consultation on Indian moccasin-making. Special thanks also to Holly Warner, Brian Burns, Geri Madden, Shirley Weiland, Les and Hop Redman, and my editor, Dinah Stevenson.

The photographs on pages 5, 38, 39, and 42 are reproduced through the courtesy of the Museum of the American Indian, Heye Foundation.

U.S. LIBRARY OF CONGRESS CATALOGING IN PUBLICATION DATA

GRAINGER, SYLVIA, BIRTH DATE
  HOW TO MAKE YOUR OWN MOCCASINS.

  BIBLIOGRAPHY: P.
  SUMMARY: DIRECTIONS FOR MAKING SOFT LEATHER FOOTWEAR IN STYLES ADAPTED FROM ORIGINAL INDIAN DESIGNS.
   1. MOCCASINS—JUVENILE LITERATURE. [1. MOCCASINS. 2. SHOES AND BOOTS] I. KRULIS, JEAN. II. TITLE.
   TT678.5.G7   746.4   77-4262
   ISBN-0-397-31754-9 ISBN-0-397-31755-7 PBK.

Contents

About This Book

Moccasins are soft leather footwear, originally made and worn by American Indians. There are many different styles: some all of soft leather for walking in the forests of the Northeast, some with stiffer soles for the harder ground of the Southwest, some high-topped for the cold Northwestern coast. The moccasins in this book are adaptations of original Indian styles. In appearance, they are very much like traditional Indian ones, but many of the pattern-making and construction techniques are different— modern tools and materials are used.

Mandan moccasins with quill decoration.

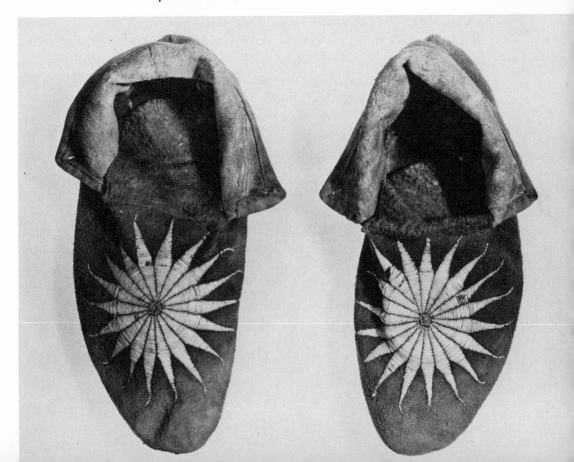

American Indian craftspeople make moccasins today, sometimes still using very old traditional methods, sometimes using newer ones. When Indian moccasin-making is mentioned in this book, it refers to traditional ways, which in some cases are still used today. (Each moccasin style in this book has an Indian name, but the name doesn't mean that no other tribe made that type of moccasin or that the tribe named didn't make other styles as well. No style is exclusive to one particular group.)

This book tells you how to make your own moccasin patterns, and how to construct moccasins using the patterns. You can choose an all soft-leather pair for indoor use, or make a style with a more sturdy sole for all-purpose wear. Moccasins are beautifully comfortable footwear, and they last a long time. When they finally need repair, you'll be able to do it yourself. And perhaps the most important reason to custom-make moccasins is to have the fun and satisfaction of creating something so useful for yourself or others.

Why make your own pattern? Not only is each foot different from every other foot, but each foot's owner also has different preferences. By drawing your own pattern, you can make your moccasins as snug or loose, high-topped or low, fringy or plain as you like. You'll have many styles—and after a little practice, many variations—to choose from.

Now a note about what you are *not* making: please don't expect moccasins to be rain galoshes. The leather can be treated for water resistance, but if you walk into a stream, the leather and your foot will get wet! (This does not ruin the leather, however.) Also, moccasins are fine for walking in the mountains—or anywhere—but they are not hiking boots, and can't be expected to offer as much protection as a heavy, thick, reinforced boot does. And one thing more: your moccasins can, with a little practice and care, be made to fit beautifully—but they are not leather stretch-stockings. Moccasins that come up high on the leg wrap around rather loosely, and are held in place with tie thongs.

Moccasin-making is easy. Most of the effort involved is in drawing the pattern; this can be accomplished by anyone with a little patience. The leatherwork is quite simple, and the directions and photos in this book will enable even a total beginner to make moccasins with a minimum of special equipment. An important key to success is taking the trouble to check the fit as you go.

How to get started? It's a good idea to read through the sections on materials and tools first, then decide which moccasins you want to make.

6

When selecting a style, keep in mind the use you will make of the moccasins. For heavy outdoor wear, a style that can have rubber soles will be better than an all-soft style, because the soles will make the moccasins wear longer and protect your feet better. If you are looking for a very simple style for your first effort, choose one of the first seven—the last three have molded soles, which take more time and equipment. The directions for making the variations are not explained as fully as the basic instructions for each style, so don't try a variation until you really understand the basic instructions—or maybe even have made the style once.

Make a pattern for the style of moccasins you have chosen. Take the pattern with you when you go to buy supplies, so you can make sure you get the right amount of leather. When you're back in your workplace, read the general directions carefully, trying out the tools and techniques on scraps of leather. Then go ahead with the moccasins.

Please look through the pattern instructions for one or two styles. You might think that the directions seem long and wordy. Don't be put off by this! In my experience, long instructions often mean clear instructions. I've tried to describe each step accurately and fully, without using symbols like "line Q-R" or "point X," since many people seem to have trouble with these. Often it will take you two seconds to locate and draw a line that I needed a whole paragraph to describe in writing. So just start at step 1, look at the illustration that goes with each step, and before long you'll be wearing your own custom-made moccasins.

Materials

Leather is the main moccasin ingredient, of course, and for the moccasins in this book you will need two kinds: soft leather for tops and for one-piece moccasins, and not-quite-so-soft leather for soles. Here are some things you need to know about leather in general.

Shape and size: Leather comes in animal shapes. Cowhides, elkhides, and sometimes calfskins are cut in half down the backbone before tanning, because tannery machines aren't big enough to handle a whole hide. Each half is called a side. Smaller skins, like sheepskins and deerskins, are left whole. The number of square feet is marked on the back. Sides of cowhide average about 20 square feet. Sides of elkhide are usually somewhat smaller, around 15 to 18 square feet, and deerskins may be anywhere from 6 to 12 square feet. Sheepskins are usually 6 to 8 square feet.

Thickness: The thickness of leather is measured, strangely enough, in ounces, and the thickness of a piece is sometimes also called its weight. The reason for this is that leather used to be measured by the number of ounces per square foot; for example, if 1 square foot of a certain leather weighed 8 ounces, it was called 8-ounce leather. This measurement has been standardized, so that "1-ounce leather" means the leather is $\frac{1}{64}''$ thick, and "8-ounce leather" is $\frac{8}{64}''$ or $\frac{1}{8}''$ thick.

> 1-ounce leather $=$ $\frac{1}{64}''$ thick
> 2-ounce leather $=$ $\frac{2}{64}''$ or $\frac{1}{32}''$ thick
> 4-ounce leather $=$ $\frac{4}{64}''$ or $\frac{1}{16}''$ thick
> 6-ounce leather $=$ $\frac{6}{64}''$ or $\frac{3}{32}''$ thick
> 8-ounce leather $=$ $\frac{8}{64}''$ or $\frac{1}{8}''$ thick

8

Unfortunately, the weight is not marked on the leather as the size is, so you'll need to ask the salesperson. With some experience, it becomes easy to tell the weight by feeling the leather.

When hides are left their original thickness and only the really thick spots are leveled off, the leather is called full grain. It has a smooth side, called the grain side (the side where the hair was), and a rough side, called the flesh side. The rough side may or may not be processed to make it evenly fuzzy (sueded). Often a hide is split down to make thinner leather; this is done by a machine with rollers and long knives called a splitter. The result is two pieces: the one with the grain side is called top-grain leather, and the bottom part, which is rough on both sides, is called a split. Top-grain leather, like full grain, has a smooth side and a rough side (which may be sueded), and though it might be quite thin (perhaps 1½-ounce) it is very strong, since much of the strength of leather is in the top grain. Split hides, of course, have no top grain left, so they are not as strong.

Usually, Indian tanning of hides involves soaking or burying them for a while, then scraping off the hair with a scraping tool. This process removes part of the top grain along with the hair. So Indian-tanned leather is usually fuzzy on both sides, like tannery-made splits, but it is stronger than split leather, because the scraping does not remove all the top grain the way splitting does. If you want your moccasins to look Indian-tanned, buy top-grain leather and use it with the rough side out, rather than buying split.

Color: Look for leather in a color you like, already dyed at the tannery. Leather and suede are available in many colors; most plentiful are beautiful browns—golden browns, reddish browns, light to dark browns. Indian-tanned leather ranges from the very light cream color of unsmoked deerskin to the rich dark brown of heavily smoked hides. Moccasins made the traditional way are never made of dyed leather, though bright-colored paints may be applied for decoration. It's not a good idea to try to dye moccasin leather yourself; it's hard to get an even color when dyeing soft leather, and dye also tends to stiffen the leather.

Tanneries color leather in two main ways. One is with dye, in a large revolving drum or vat. The dye soaks right into the grain of the leather, making a natural-looking surface with the grain still showing. The other usual way to color leather is with a flexible paint. The paint is usually sprayed onto the leather and does not soak in, but stays right on the surface, covering up most of the grain. I don't recommend this kind of leather for moccasins, because it looks almost like plastic—too shiny and perfect.

SOFT LEATHER FOR TOPS AND ONE-PIECE MOCCASINS

The leather used for moccasin tops and for one-piece moccasins should be soft and pliable. Historically Indians have used many kinds of animal skins—buffalo, elk, deer, moose, reindeer—and they made the leather very soft by oiling the hide, stretching it out, and rubbing it for a long time with a tool made of stone, bone, or wood. Then the hide might be smoked over a fire of wet or rotten wood to turn it a darker brown, make it last longer, and keep it soft. If you are interested in the details of Indian tanning or would even like to try it yourself, see the book list on page 128 for some good sources of information.

Modern tanneries make soft leather by a process known as "chrome tanning," or tanning with chromium salts. You'll be able to tell a chrome-tanned piece, because if you pick it up and drop it it flops into a heap instead of keeping a flat stiff shape. Chrome-tanned leather can be thick or thin, and the flesh side may or may not be sueded.

Nearly every supplier sells chrome-tanned cowhide with both the smooth and the sueded sides usable. Sometimes deerskin and elkhide are available; it's easy to spot them because of the shapes and the supersoft feel of the skins. Sheepskin is usually too thin for moccasin-making, except for a special kind of sheepskin called shearling—it has the wool left on, sheared down to an even length, with the other side sueded. Osage style moccasins (page 94) are easily made out of shearling. It's also possible to make other styles of moccasins out of shearling, but the patterns would have to be made larger to allow for the extra room the wool takes up.

Many supply stores have leather called "buck-tanned" or "deer-tanned." These are cowhide tanned to resemble buckskin or deerskin; the color is usually golden brown or yellow gold; the skins are very soft and somewhat stretchy. They are excellent for moccasins.

Ask for chrome-tanned leather or suede that is from 2 to 5 ounces in weight. This is quite a range, and it's mostly a matter of taste what thickness you use, but under 2 ounces probably wouldn't be strong enough for moccasins. The style you are making may affect your choice; for example, high-topped moccasins would probably be too bulky if made with 5-ounce leather. It also depends on the use you'll make of your moccasins: for indoor slipper wear, you might want thinner leather than for outside, shoe-type use. The leather does not have to be very thick to be strong and long-lasting, however, as long as it has one smooth top-grain side.

Chrome-tanned leather and suede usually cost a little less than other, stiffer types, probably between $1.25 and $2 per square foot.

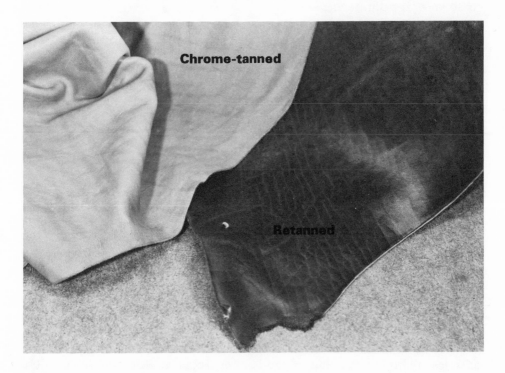

NOT-QUITE-SO-SOFT LEATHER FOR SOLES

The moccasins worn by many Eastern Woodland Indians have soft soles made of the same leather as the tops, while those of the Plains and Southwestern Indians have flat or molded soles of thicker leather. The forest floor was probably softer to walk on than the ground of the other areas, and feet required less protection.

Some of the moccasins in this book have flat or shaped soles of thicker leather. The best leather for this purpose is called retanned cowhide, because it is chrome-tanned and then tanned again (*re*-tanned) by a process called oak tanning. Oak-tanned leather is stiff; it can also be formed into a shape when it is wet, and it will keep that shape when it dries. Cowhide that has been *only* oak-tanned would be too stiff and uncomfortable for moccasin soles. Retanned cowhide has some oil and wax in it, so it's easy to work with, lasts a long time, and is comfortable to wear. At first, ask to see oak-tanned, chrome-tanned, and retanned leather; after a while you'll get to know the difference.

If your style requires thicker leather soles, get a piece of retanned cowhide the color you want, and between 4 and 6 ounces in weight. It is possible to use still heavier leather for soles, and some people like to, but leather that isn't over 6 ounces is easier to work with, especially if you are making molded soles. Retanned cowhide usually costs around $1.50 to $2.50 per square foot.

Latigo (LAT-ago) is the name of a certain kind of retanned cowhide that is a favorite with craftspeople for belts, bags, and many other projects— it's often dyed yellow at the tannery. Latigo would work for moccasin-sole leather except that it is usually too thick. If you can find 4-to-5- or 5-to-6-ounce latigo, fine. The leather shown in this book is 5-to-6-ounce medium brown retanned cowhide called "shoe leather" by the tannery that makes it.

When Indians made moccasin soles of leather different from that in the tops, they used either heavier leather (perhaps buffalo hide) or, more often, rawhide (untanned hides). To make rawhide, the hides (again, often buffalo, until buffalo became scarce) were stretched out, either on a frame of poles or staked out just off the ground. Flesh and hair were scraped off, and when the hide had dried in the sun for several days, it could be used for soles, thongs, bags, rattles, and many other useful and ornamental things. Some groups, especially in the Plains, made large rawhide bags for holding all sorts of things, particularly dried meat. These bags were called "parfleches" (par-FLESH) by the Europeans. When a bag wore out in spots (after a long time!) it might be cut up to make moccasin soles, so rawhide soles are often called parfleche soles.

Rawhide soles had certain advantages for Indian moccasin-makers: they were very tough, so they would last and protect the feet, and rawhide was easy to make compared to tanned leather. But for our purposes, I recommend retanned cowhide. Rawhide is extremely difficult to work with because it is so hard and stiff (almost impossible to get a needle through); it's not easy to find, except in the pet shop as dog bones; it is hard on the feet; and finally, it's slippery when wet!

WHERE AND HOW TO BUY

The best place to look for moccasin-making leather, tools, and other necessities is in a store that specializes in leatherwork supplies. These stores are listed under LEATHER in the yellow pages of the phone book, and there is a list of suppliers in the back of this book. Leatherworking supplies are not standardized items; not every supplier has the same things. So you may have to shop around to find exactly what you want, or get some supplies by mail order.

Leather is usually sold by the whole piece—that is, by the side or hide. The price is figured by the square foot. Prices might range from $1.25 to $2.50 per square foot, so a side of cowhide might be around $40, a deerskin $20, a shearling $14—there is a lot of variation. A whole piece is more than you will need for one pair of moccasins (a side of cowhide might be enough for eight to ten pairs), so you may want to shop around to find a supplier who is willing to sell you less than that. If the shop will cut you a smaller piece, the price per square foot will probably go up, since the remaining piece may be harder for them to sell. If you can't find a place that sells less than a whole side or hide, try getting together with other moccasin-makers to share supplies.

There is only one way to tell how much leather you need, and that is to take the pattern with you when you go to buy the leather, even if you plan to buy a large piece. Then you can fit the pieces on the hide to make sure the shape of the hide will work for your pattern. Also, if you take your pattern, the people at the store will be able to help you get the best leather for your project. If you are buying by mail order, you could make a copy of your pattern and send it with the order.

It's difficult to estimate the cost of leather for your moccasin project, since there is so much variation—in the price of the leather you choose, the size of your feet, the style of moccasin—but a very rough guess is that leather for one pair could cost from $4 to $15.

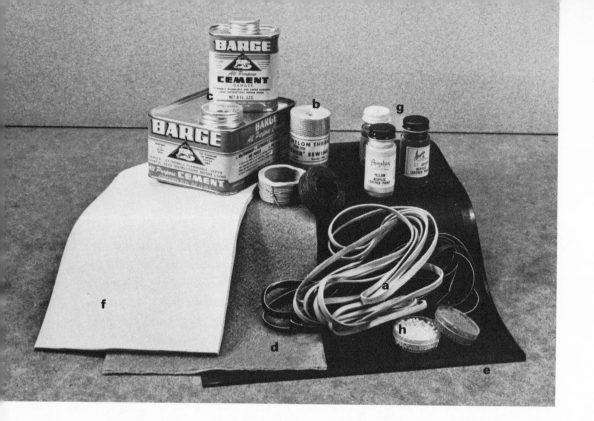

THONGS

A narrow strip of leather called a thong or lace is used on most moccasins, to help hold them on. Thongs (a) can be bought already cut, sometimes in strips of several feet, sometimes by the foot in whatever length you need. One-quarter inch is a good width, since thongs tend to stretch out with use, and narrower thongs aren't strong enough. The thongs may or may not match the leather of the moccasin tops, but they should be chrome-tanned for flexibility. Check the style you're going to make to see how much you need. Thongs usually cost around 10¢ per foot. It is quite easy to cut your own thongs from the leather you use for the moccasin tops, even if you don't have much left over—if you want to do it yourself, just allow an inch or so extra when you buy the leather.

THREAD

Indian moccasin makers sewed with animal sinew (strong fibers connecting muscle to bone), or sometimes strips of rawhide, until thread became available from traders. The best thing for the modern moccasin-maker is heavy waxed nylon thread (b), which is sold in small quantities at leather-supply stores; it comes in black, brown, white, and natural (light tan).

14

This thread costs about 75¢ to $1 for a 25- to 30-yard roll, and that's more than enough for two pairs.

GLUE

I highly recommend rubber cement for keeping thread knots secure. You'll also need cement if you plan to use a rubber bottom sole. Rubber contact cement (c) can be found at leather-supply stores and shoe-repair shops. The very best kind is Atco Tan Label brand, but this is usually sold by the gallon only! The next best is Barge Cement—it works fine. The can (8 ounces, about $2.50, or 1 quart, about $4.50) is very convenient, because there is a brush in the can lid. If you want to buy only enough glue for one pair, get a small tube (2 ounces, $1). The larger sizes, of course, are more economical. Avoid the kind of rubber cement used for gluing paper; it is not strong enough to hold leather.

RUBBER SOLES

A rubber sole glued onto the leather sole is optional on some styles, and it's a good idea. Indians obviously didn't use rubber soles, but they didn't have any—and they weren't walking on concrete surfaces all day. Leather is wonderful, but rubber gives better traction, especially when the ground is wet. Rubber wears better, too, and can add a little comforting cushion between the foot and the floor or the ground.

For styles that have flat, stitched-on soles of retanned cowhide, some sort of glued-on bottom layer is essential to keep the stitching from rubbing on the ground and wearing out. If you don't want a rubber sole, glue on an extra layer of leather instead.

On moccasins made entirely of soft leather, rubber soles may be too stiff, and you will probably not want to use them. You can use soft leather as an extra sole layer on soft moccasins; then the sole can be replaced easily when necessary.

If you decide to use a rubber sole, choose a material that is easy to cut, relatively thin (about ⅛″ or less), and flexible. Two good kinds are Malaya crepe (d) and "galosh" (e) (used on the bottom of galoshes). Rubber soling can be found in a leather-supply store or a shoe-repair shop. It comes in rectangles that you cut to shape yourself, and is priced at around $2 for a piece big enough to make two soles.

SPONGE INSOLES

I recommend a layer of $\frac{3}{16}''$ orthopedic sponge rubber (f) cut to the foot outline and slipped inside the moccasin. This makes the moccasins very comfortable; once you try it you'll never leave it out! It's possible to glue in the insole, but it will stay in place fine without glue, and then you can take it out and wash it. If you get real orthopedic sponge rubber (not cheap foam), the insole will take the shape of your foot and give it some support. Orthopedic sponge may be available where you buy your leather; if not, look for it in a shoe-repair shop or in an orthopedic appliance store. It will cost $1 to $1.50 for enough for one pair of insoles.

DECORATING MATERIALS

If you decide to paint designs on your moccasins, get some acrylic leather paint (g) where you buy the other supplies. It should be special leather paint so it will be flexible and not crack or come off. The paint comes in many colors, and a little goes a long way. It costs about 90¢ for a 1-ounce bottle, which is enough for many pairs of moccasins. If you want many colors but don't want to buy a lot of bottles of paint, you can buy primary colors (red, blue, yellow), plus white and black, perhaps, and mix other colors.

Most beading is done with tiny ($\frac{1}{8}''$ by $\frac{1}{16}''$) beads called seed beads (h). These can be found at hobby and general craft shops. For beading, you'll also need regular sewing thread (cotton will do, but polyester or nylon is stronger) and some wax for the thread—beeswax, paraffin, even a candle end will do.

COST OF MATERIALS

It's easy to see that moccasin-making is more economical when several pairs are planned—almost everything you need is less expensive in larger amounts than are needed for one pair. The cost will also be affected by the options you choose, of course. It makes a difference whether your style uses a lot of leather or a little, whether you decide to buy sponge, decorations, etc. The materials for the first pair will probably total $10 to $20. This is still a lot less than the cost of a pair of good-quality custom-made moccasins!

Tools

Moccasins can be made with surprisingly few tools. Besides the pattern-making aids, the essentials are something to cut with, a punch, and a needle. Other tools may be necessary in some cases, so check with the directions as you make a shopping list. For example, if you want to make a pair of moccasins with molded soles, you'll need a saw to cut out the wooden form with. Leatherworking tools can be bought from leather-supply stores.

FOR PATTERN-MAKING

You'll need a large piece of paper for pattern-making. I like a piece of brown wrapping paper at least two feet square, such as a large smooth grocery bag cut open, but most any kind will do as long as it's not really flimsy. Don't try to use notebook-sized paper. If you are going to make the Navajo or Apache styles, which include full-size printed patterns, you'll need tracing paper too. Also collect a pencil, scissors, ruler, tape measure, and T-square. If you don't have a T-square, find something to draw square corners with, like a box or a piece of cardboard—anything that definitely makes a right angle you can draw around. Of course, the tribal moccasin-maker of the last century didn't use a drafting table filled with these goodies! However, an Indian group rarely made more than one or two styles of footwear, and the craftsperson had the benefit of the group's long experience with the pattern.

FOR CUTTING

A simple single-edged razor in a holder (a) works very well to cut all of the materials—leather, rubber, and sponge. The razor cutter costs about 70¢, and extra blades can be purchased in a package of eight, also 70¢ or so. It's a good idea to cover your work table with something like a piece of Masonite or plywood so it won't be damaged by the cutter.

Leather shears (b) are an alternative way to cut; they are expensive (around $13) but easier to use and more convenient than the cutter. A good brand will cut all kinds of leather—soft or stiff, thick or thin. Try out the shears before buying them, if at all possible. One excellent brand (my favorite) is Marks' Serra-Sharp.

FOR MARKING EVEN STITCHES

The stitchmarker (c) is an optional tool, except for making the Penobscot style, where it's essential. It has a wooden handle and a little pointed wheel that is pressed along the leather and marks the position of the sewing holes. It's handy and not expensive (about $1.75)—get the 6-to-the-inch one. For soft-leather-only moccasins, where you won't need to punch holes, a stitchmarker is not necessary.

If you'd rather not buy a stitchmarker, you can gauge the distance between sewing holes by eye, measure with a ruler and mark the points with a pencil, or use the tines of a dinner fork as markers.

FOR PUNCHING

Check the directions for the style you want to make to see what punch, if any, you will need. Some moccasins are sewn together with a sharp needle and don't require a punch at all. If you do need to punch sewing holes, get a spring (squeeze-type) punch (d), size #00 ($\frac{1}{32}''$). Spring punches cost about $3. On styles where a thong is used, a bigger hole is needed. For thong holes, get a #5 ($\frac{9}{64}''$), #6 ($\frac{5}{32}''$), or #7 ($\frac{3}{16}''$) spring punch. I use the #7, but keep in mind when choosing that a #5 or #6 punch is more useful in general leatherwork, because it punches rivet- and lacing-sized holes. If you have a small (#00) punch and would rather not buy a larger punch for thong holes, try punching many little holes with the small punch to make a big hole.

In early times, holes for sewing and thongs were made with awls of sharpened stone, bone, or thorn. In the Southwest, cactus "needles" were sometimes used. Later, metal awl points and needles did the job.

The rotary punch, with different-sized tubes on a wheel, is tempting—it offers you several sizes of hole for about twice the cost of a single-tube punch—but I don't recommend it. Even if you do other leather projects, most likely you'll still only need the small sewing size (#00) and a larger all-purpose size. Most rotary punches don't go smaller than #0, which is one size too large. And, unfortunately, the rotary punch isn't a very good tool. Often the wheel slips out of position as you try to punch. Also, different-sized punches chew up the little copper anvil, so the punch won't cut a nice clean hole.

FOR SEWING

A paper stapler is necessary for fitting the Shawnee, Winnebago, and Flathead styles; you may want to use it when sewing seams on other styles as well.

Get a size #00 glover's needle (e) for sewing the moccasins together. This needle has a sharp, three-sided point, and it's about 2″ long. A smaller one might seem better because it makes a smaller hole in the leather, but the #00 is much easier to use. Usually the needles can be bought either singly (for around 15¢) or in packages of 25 (for around $2.50). They last a long time—I've never known one to break—so just get one unless you tend to lose needles.

For the Penobscot style, dull-pointed needles called harness needles are used, since the holes are already punched in both pieces to be sewn. Large ones are easier to handle than small; get two of size #000.

FOR TAPPING SEAMS AND GLUED AREAS

A metal hammer and anvil (f) come in handy for flattening seams and glued areas. Any hammer will do, if the tapping surface is clean and smooth so it won't damage the leather. You can use a real anvil or any heavy metal object that you can tap on—a vise, a big hammer turned on its side, the flat part of an axe, a heavy frying pan. You don't absolutely have to have these tools, but flattened seams look nicer and are usually more comfortable, and glued surfaces stick better if they're tapped together.

FOR MAKING MOLDED SOLES

If the style you choose has molded soles, you'll need to make a wooden mold. For this purpose you'll need some plywood. Get one or two pieces, depending on whether you're going to make one or two molds (see page 30). Get a piece of ½″ thick plywood 2″ bigger than your foot all around. For example, if your foot measures 3″ wide and 9″ long, the wood should be 7″ wide and 13″ long.

You will need a drill to make a hole in the plywood to start the cut, and you'll need some sort of saw to cut out the foot shape with. A hand or electric drill will make the hole, which should be big enough for you to get the saw blade into. A ½″ drill is a good size, unless you're using a bigger saw blade. The hole can be *bigger* than the saw blade without causing any problem.

Plywood is easy to cut, and you can use a coping saw, saber saw, jigsaw, or hacksaw. It has to be a saw that you can guide around the foot shape easily, and one that can start the cut from your drilled hole rather than from the edge of the wood.

If you have neither a saw nor a friend with a saw, have a look at a hardware store or lumber yard. You can buy a coping saw for around $2. If you really don't want to buy one, ask the lumber yard if they'll make the hole and cut for you. Sometimes they will do it, but the charge will almost certainly be more than the price of a coping saw.

Also get a piece of sandpaper to smooth the edges of your wooden form with. It really doesn't matter what kind. A file will work, too. Finally, you'll need a C-clamp to hold the wood to the bench while you drill and cut.

FOR DECORATING

Painted decorations require a small paintbrush; size depends on the size of the areas to be painted. Cheap dime-store paintbrushes will work, but it's a little harder to do fine work with them, since the brush hairs fall out over a period of time. I like a Grumbacher #815 camel-hair brush, size #0 for tiny lines, size #3 for small areas, size #6 for large areas. Try the #3 at first. These brushes can be found in art-supply and craft shops. They cost around $1.50 each.

An electric pen or wood-burning tool is great for decorating. These pens are sold by craft and hobby shops, hardware stores, and some leather suppliers. Usually the price is $6 or so, although if the tool comes in a set including wood projects, it will probably cost more.

For beading, get some size #7 glover's needles. These needles are 1½″ long, small enough to go through seed beads, and sharp enough to pierce leather easily. It's a good idea to buy several, for the overlay beading stitch requires two at a time, and the needles are so tiny that they are easily mislaid. Glover's needles can usually be found in leather-supply stores. They cost about 15¢ each.

COST OF TOOLS

If you already have pattern-making supplies, you can make moccasins with an expenditure of $4 or less for a razor cutter, punch, and needle. The rest is optional—shears, larger punch, stitchmarker, saw, decorating tools, etc.

How to Make Moccasins

THE PATTERN

The first step in moccasin-making, as I mentioned before, is to make the pattern so you can take it along when you go leather shopping. If you plan to use a sponge-rubber insole, take a foot outline along too, so you can tell how much sponge to buy.

The reason for drawing your own pattern is to insure a real custom fit by constructing it around the shape and size of *your* foot. Each pattern starts with a foot outline (see below) and requires at least one additional measurement. The more accurately you measure, the better the moccasins are likely to fit. (I don't recommend making a pair as a surprise for someone unless you have found a way to measure feet secretly!)

The pattern instructions have been designed for a snug fit wherever possible, so that the moccasins will stay on your feet, and because leather stretches somewhat when it is worn. If you plan to wear heavy socks with the moccasins, draw the foot outline and take all measurements with the socks on. You do *not* have to allow extra room for ease unless you want your moccasins loose and floppy.

FOOT MEASUREMENTS

To draw a foot outline: Place your right foot on the paper, leaving plenty of space around the foot on all sides for the rest of the pattern. Put your weight on the foot, because the foot may be larger with your weight on it, and draw around it with a soft pencil. Keep the pencil vertical—upright—as you outline the foot, so that the line doesn't dip way in under the foot along the arch. Make a smooth curve along the toes.

22

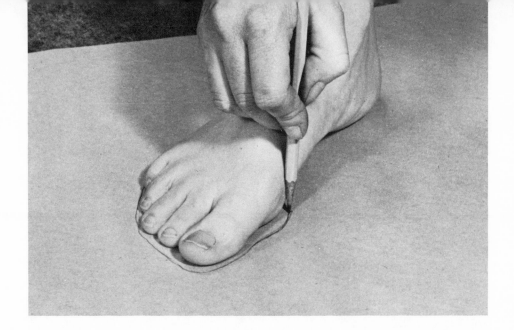

To measure the perimeter of the foot: Measure the distance around the edge of the foot outline. This can be done with a tape measure, but it's easier to be accurate if you place a piece of string or thread carefully around the outline and then measure the length of the string or thread.

To measure the arch: There are three different methods. Check the directions for your style to see which measurement you need.

All the way around the arch: Place the tape measure on the drawing, on the point specified in the directions. Put your foot on the drawing and wrap the tape measure all the way around your foot. Hold the end of the tape measure at the top of your foot so that you can read the measurement.

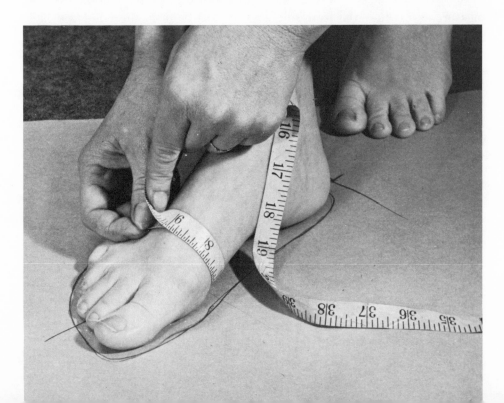

Over the arch to the floor: Put your foot on the drawing. With a tape measure, measure from the floor on one side over the arch to the floor on the other side, at the point specified in the directions.

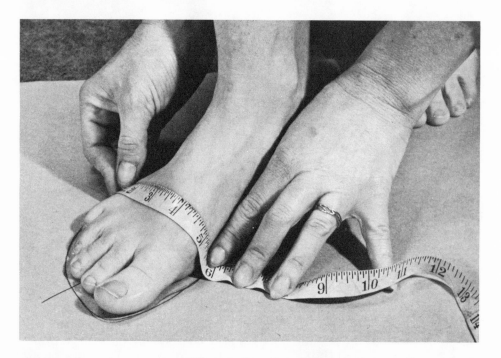

Over the arch to the molded sole: Place the molded sole on the drawing so that you can see where to measure. Put your foot in the molded sole and measure across the arch from sole edge to sole edge at the point specified in the directions.

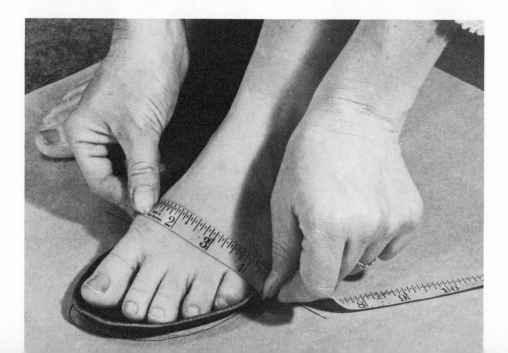

To measure from the toe to the beginning of the leg bend: Measure on the foot from the end of your longest toe to the point at which your leg starts to curve upward.

DRAWING THE LINES

To draw a heel-toe line: Measure the width of the foot outline at the ankle, and put a pencil dot at the midpoint. Do the same at the widest part of the foot. Connect the dots, using a ruler, to make a line from heel to toe in the middle of the foot. Extend the line several inches beyond the heel and toe, in case you need to mark points there.

To draw a perpendicular line: A perpendicular line is a line at right angles to another line. To draw a perpendicular line at a given point on another line, place the T-square along the original line with the corner at that given point, and draw the new line.

To draw a parallel line: Parallel lines are always the same distance apart. To draw a parallel line a given distance from another line, measure that distance from the first line at several points along the line, and make dots. Connect the dots.

To center a measurement on a line: You'll have a line with a point marked on it, and a measurement to be centered. Divide the measurement in half and mark a point on the line *this* distance from the original point. Mark another point the same distance away from the original point on the other side. If the measurement is 3″, for example, mark two points each 1½″ away from the first point.

For the Navajo and Apache styles, you'll be drawing part of the pattern and then adding it to a printed pattern that you'll find with the directions for the style. Trace the printed pattern onto a piece of paper, cut it out, and draw around it to incorporate it into the pattern you have made.

After drawing your pattern, cut the pieces out. You might cut out enough paper pattern pieces for both feet as well as for any other pairs you're going to make, so you can plan the layout on the leather for everything at once. Some patterns are symmetrical—the same on both sides; that is, if the pattern is folded down the center line, the halves match, and the left moccasin will be the same as the right. But more commonly the halves do not match, and then the right foot pattern must be different from the left. Cutting out two left or two right feet is a very common mistake, and not only among beginners; so, to be safe, cut out two paper pattern pieces and mark them "right" and "left."

Should you make a pattern for one foot and turn it over for the other foot, or make two separate patterns, one for right and one for left? This is up to you. If your feet are pretty much the same shape (compare foot out-lines), just make one pattern. If they are significantly different, it's better to make two. The pattern-making instructions are based on a right-foot outline, so be sure to reverse sides to make a left-foot pattern. The wooden form for molded soles can also be made once and reversed if the right and left feet are reasonably similar in size and shape.

Feet are strangely shaped things, and, while constructing moccasins to fit them just right isn't terribly hard, it takes some care. If you have an unusually high arch, for example, there's an increased chance that you'll have to adjust the pattern. Keep checking the pattern and then the leather pieces for fit every chance you get—I do it at every step. When you have drawn the pattern and cut it out, you can check it by holding it on the foot and carefully taping the pieces together. Even better, cut the pattern pieces out of cloth (felt is good) and baste them together with needle and thread. Remember that paper and cloth don't take up as much room as the leather will, so the pattern will be just a little looser than the real moccasins.

Keep the paper pattern pieces after use, in case you want another pair in that style. It's a good idea to write notes on them about possible improvements or things to try the next time.

CUTTING

Spread the leather out on a flat surface. Decide which side of the leather (top grain or sueded) you want for the "out" side, and lay the leather with that side showing. If you plan to paint a design on the moccasins, use the top-grain side showing, as suede is too rough to hold the paint.

Look the leather over thoroughly as you lay out the pattern pieces. Check both sides, avoiding cuts, holes, and very thin, weak, or stretchy places. Also look for scratches and brands, although you can use these areas if there aren't actual holes. Leather does have interesting markings and grain patterns that will add to the beauty of your moccasins. The direction of placement does not matter. You can fit the pieces in in any direction, and put them as close together as possible to use the leather economically.

When the pieces are all placed, check to make sure you have allowed for right and left where necessary. Then weight the pattern down with heavy objects like books, an anvil, etc., and draw around each piece with a soft pencil. Move the pencil back and forth slowly if it doesn't mark readily; you just need a light line to cut on. Don't use pen, because ink cannot be removed, and the line would show.

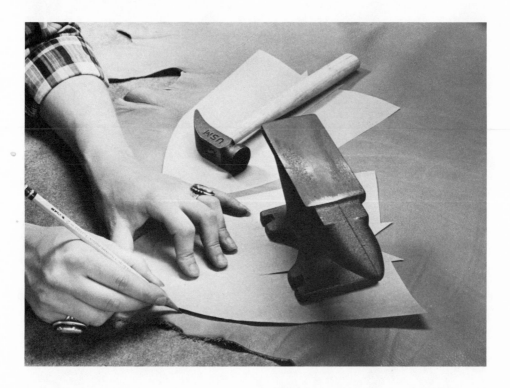

Now, take away the paper and prepare to cut out the leather pieces. Cutting with the razor cutter is easiest when the blade is relatively new and unchipped, so check it often and put in a new blade when necessary. Practice cutting a scrap first. With the leather on a flat cutting surface, sink the blade through the leather and into the cutting table. Pull on the *leather*, and hold the cutter still. It's easier to control the cut when you pull on the leather rather than the cutter, and you cannot cut yourself, since your hand is never in front of the cutting edge of the razor. Pull the leather slowly, and keep moving your pulling hand back to the cutter. Cut out each pattern piece right on the line.

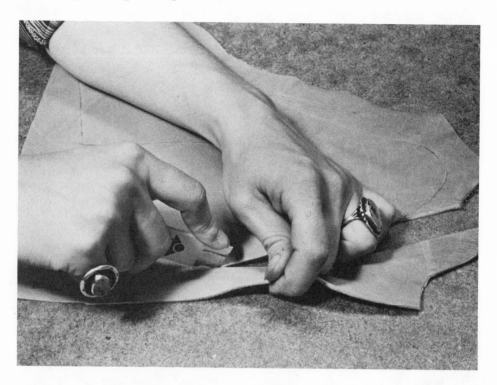

Leather shears work just like paper scissors except that they are very sharp, so use caution. Make a few practice cuts on scrap to get the feel of the shears before cutting out the pattern pieces.

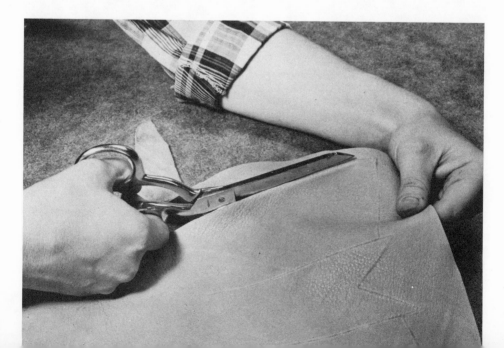

Cutting your own thongs is easy. It can be done with shears or a razor cutter; shears are more convenient. The thong strips should be about ¼″ wide. At first, measure the ¼″ width with a ruler and draw a pencil guideline for cutting. After a while, you'll be able to do it by eye. Thongs do not have to come off a straight piece—you can cut them from just about any curve, even from a small circular piece of leather, in a spiral. They will straighten out when gently stretched, or gradually, with use. Cut points or tapered ends on the thongs so they'll look nice and go through the holes easily. (You might cut extra thongs to save in case the others get lost or worn out.)

Keep some pieces of scrap for later repairs.

If you've decided to have a sponge insole, you can cut that now too. Draw around the paper foot outline—you can use either pencil or pen this time, since it won't show—and cut out the sponge using regular scissors, leather shears, or a razor cutter. Cut either right on the line or just inside the line so the sponge won't be too big to fit inside the moccasin easily.

MOLDED SOLES

Some of the moccasin styles have firm soles that are formed around a piece of wood. The molded sole curves up around the foot so that the seam joining it to the upper part is about ½″ off the ground. The leather is shaped in a mold that consists of two pieces of wood—a foot-shaped piece and a piece with a larger foot-shaped hole in it. The leather is pushed into

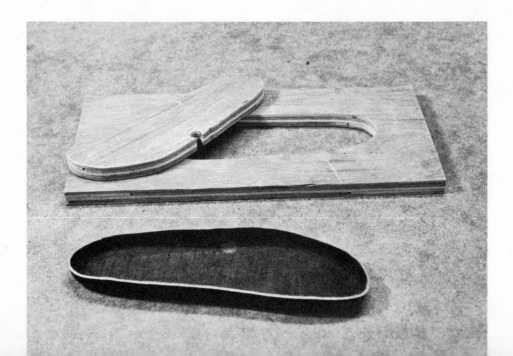

the hole while wet and is held in place till dry by the foot-shaped piece. This method of forming soles works very well, and produces a sole that looks good and is easy to work with. I have never seen or heard of Indian soles formed in quite this way—sometimes the rawhide is wet and bent up with the fingers, with or without an object to press against.

For these soles, cut two rectangular pieces of retanned cowhide, each one with a 2″ margin around the foot outline on all sides. For example, if your foot measures 3″ wide and 9″ long, make each rectangle of leather 7″ wide and 13″ long.

Then prepare the mold. Place your foot on a piece of ½″ thick plywood, leaving at least two inches between the foot and the edge of the wood on all sides. Draw a foot outline (see page 22). Draw the other foot on paper, cut out the paper, and check to see if the feet are similar in size and shape —if they are, you can use one mold for both feet.

Clamp the plywood to a workbench and drill a hole through the wood. Put this hole on the inside of the foot outline, within the foot shape, on a relatively straight side of the foot—not right on the toe or heel. The toe and heel are tight curves, and all of the wood is necessary there to press the leather into place.

With a saw, cut out the foot shape. To use a jigsaw, coping saw, or hacksaw, take the blade out of the saw, put it in the drilled hole, and replace

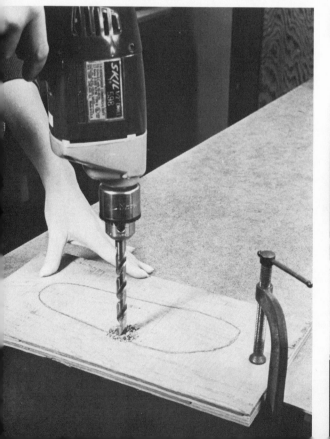
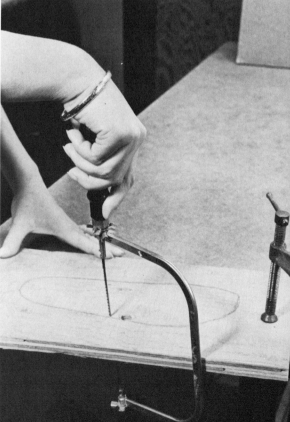

it in the saw so you can start the cut. Saber-saw blades are only attached at one end, so the blade can be set into the hole without being removed from the saw. Make the cut just on the *inside* of the pencil line, so that the line remains on the outside part of the wood. You'll need to change the position of the wood as you cut; you'll find yourself reclamping it several times as you go around the foot.

The leather is about 5 ounces in thickness, or $\frac{5}{64}''$ thick, so it's necessary to have a space of about $\frac{8}{64}''$, or $\frac{1}{8}''$, between the outside part of the mold and the foot shape so the leather will fit. If you have too much space, the mold will still work, but if there is too little, you won't be able to get the leather and wood into place. Saw blades remove a little bit of wood as they cut, but not enough to allow for the thickness of the leather. Clamp the wood to the bench and trim away about $\frac{1}{8}''$ from the outside part of the mold to make this space, using the saw. It helps to measure the $\frac{1}{8}''$ with a ruler and make a pencil guideline. This trimming could be done with a file, but that would take a long time!

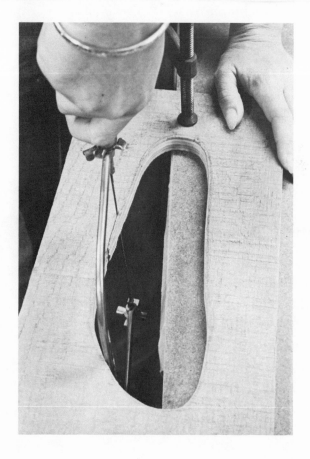

Next set the foot shape in the outside part and check to make sure that there is enough space for the leather. Smooth the edges of both parts of the mold with sandpaper so that the leather won't be scratched.

Now you're ready to form the sole. Soak the leather piece in water until it's thoroughly wet; you can put it in a plastic bag with water. Leave it for about 20 minutes—the exact time is not critical. Shake off excess water. With the smooth, grain side *down*, put the leather in the outside part of the mold and push it down into the mold with your fingers. Press in the foot shape. If it doesn't go in easily, you can tap on it with a hammer, but don't pound hard or the wood might break. I put mine on the floor and step on the foot shape to make it go in all the way. If you really can't get it in, you'll have to trim the mold more to allow for the thickness of the leather.

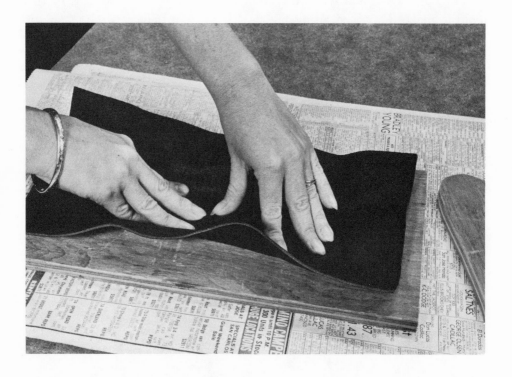

Prop the mold up off the table so air can circulate around the leather, and let it dry at least overnight. Put it in the sun for a while if you can; a little warmth and sunlight "bake" the leather into shape nicely. If the foot shape holds the leather in loosely, put a weight on the wood to press it into place.

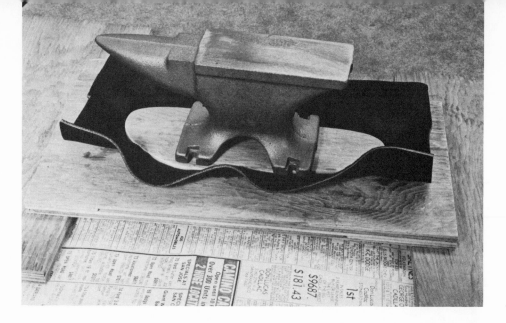

When the leather is thoroughly dry, take it out of the mold. Using a razor cutter or shears, cut off the excess leather, leaving a turned-up rim about ½″ high (that should be just the amount shaped by the mold, since the plywood is ½″ thick). The trimming is easier with shears, but a razor cutter works fine if you cut slowly and carefully, with the molded sole on its side, holding the leather by the excess part. Put in your foot, to try out the fit.

For the other foot, *reverse the mold by turning it upside down,* and repeat the process. If you made two molds, of course, you can do both soles at once, but be sure you have the molds turned the correct side up so that you'll end up with one right and one left!

Keep the mold, because it can be used over and over again as long as your feet stay the same size—you needn't make a new mold for every pair.

PUNCHING

Moccasin pieces made of chrome-tanned leather are sewn with a sharp glover's needle, and holes are not punched in the leather first. But retanned cowhide soles, molded or flat, need sewing holes. It's certainly possible to push a glover's needle through this leather, but it is difficult to do, and it's hard to make an evenly spaced seam this way.

The Indians have always sewn parfleche (rawhide) soles in a special way. The hide is so thick that the awl or needle can be pushed into the *side* edge and come out the *top*, rather than going all the way through the hide. This way, the stitches do not rub on the ground, and do not show.

33

Try stitching like that on a piece of thick cowhide to appreciate the strength and skill it must take—and rawhide is much harder to work with than tanned leather!

To mark points for evenly spaced holes, run a 6-to-the-inch stitchmarker along the edge of the sole on the top-grain side. The points should be ⅛″ from the edge; measure the ⅛″ with a ruler and draw a light pencil guideline for the stitchmarker. If you don't have a stitchmarker, you can measure the distance between points with the ruler and mark the dots with a pencil. For molded soles, put the wooden foot shape of the mold into the leather sole while you mark the position of the sewing holes so there will be something solid to back up the leather.

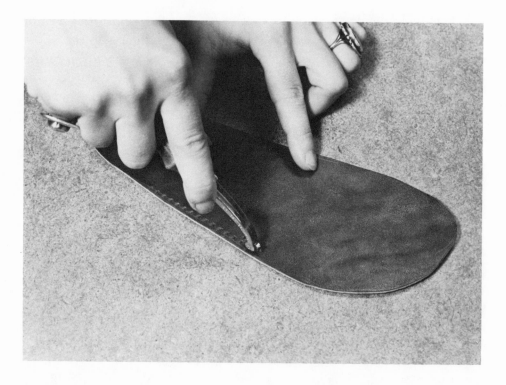

Use a #00 spring punch to punch one hole at each marked point. Sometimes a new punch won't cut the hole out cleanly; it will get better with use. If you have any trouble, try twisting the punch sideways as you squeeze, to help the cutting edge clean out the hole. The bits of leather will fall out the other end of the punch tube; you don't have to pick them out.

34

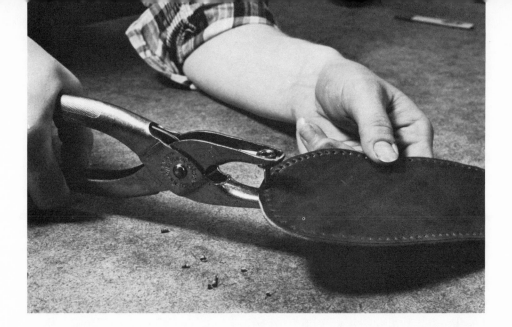

A spring punch will last for many years and never need sharpening if the punch tube does not get damaged. To keep yours in fine shape, hang it up when you're not using it so it won't get dropped or have something fall on it and chip the tube. You can keep it closed with a rubber band around the handle so that the cutting end of the punch is not exposed. If the punch tube does get damaged, you can buy a new one separately and install it in the punch.

Tie-thong holes are punched after the moccasins are sewn up so that you can tell where you want them. Use a bigger punch (#5, #6, or #7) or nibble out a big hole by making several small ones. If the soft leather seems difficult to punch, try punching some holes in a scrap of harder leather, to break in the punch; or you can put the soft leather you want to punch on top of a piece of harder scrap and punch through the soft leather into the hard leather.

DECORATING

Decorating should be done before the pieces are sewn together, while they are still flat. Of course, this is an optional step—decorated moccasins are nice, but plain ones are beautiful too.

DESIGNS

There are a great many choices of designs. You can draw your own or consult a book for ideas; the book list on page 128 includes several suggested starting places. Keep the shape of the pieces as well as the method of decoration in mind as you look at designs. Feel free to pick anything you like —floral, geometric, American Indian or other folk designs, for example. If you would like your moccasins to be decorated in a traditional way, look through one or more of the books on Indian designs, or go to the library for books on particular tribes, and match the type of design with the style of your moccasins. You can even use the special colors the group would have used if you like.

To transfer a design to the leather, draw or trace it on a piece of paper, using a soft pencil. Turn the paper upside down and place it on the leather. Rub the pencil over the paper, scribbling lines that cover the design area. The lines of the design will be marked on the moccasin piece. Notice that this technique makes the design come out backward. If that matters—for

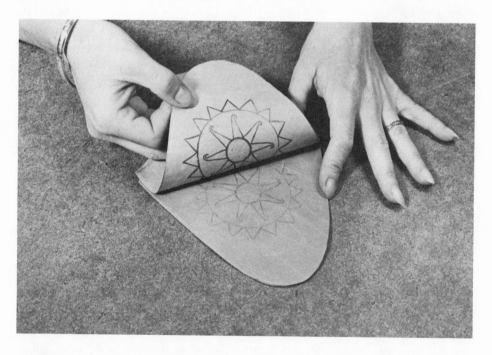

instance, with a design that includes letters—you can use the technique in two steps: trace or draw as usual, but do it heavily enough that the lines show through the paper. Turn the paper over and trace the design on the opposite side, turn it back, and place it on the leather. Transfer the design as above.

Some Eastern Woodland moccasin-makers used birchbark design patterns that they saved to use again and again; sometimes they cut these templates by biting the bark with their teeth.

ELECTRIC PEN

The electric pen or wood-burning tool makes an attractive light brown line on the leather. The pen makes the line shrink down very slightly, raising the area around it and giving the design a three-dimensional quilted effect—a bit bumpy, and very nice. It works better on some leathers than others (and not at all well on suede), so you have to try it out on scrap first. Check the instructions that come with the pen to see how long it takes to warm up. Also check to see what areas on the pen are hot—these places get hot enough to burn fingers!

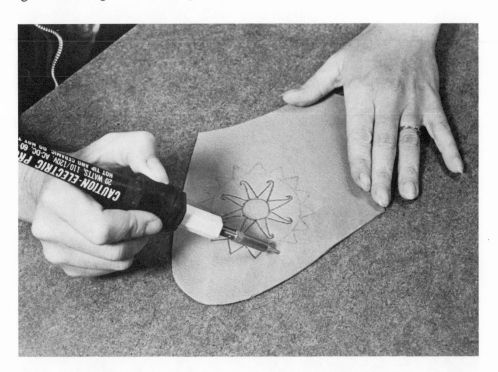

Used by itself, the electric pen makes a pleasantly subtle decoration; you can also use it to outline areas for painting. Some Indian groups outlined designs by burning with a heated stone or piece of bone.

PAINT

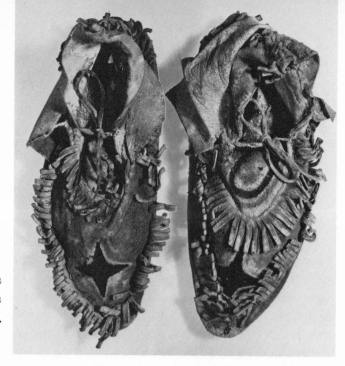

Arapaho deerskin moccasins with painted decoration.

Many tribes have traditionally used paints to decorate their moccasins. Before Europeans came to trade, bringing brightly colored paints, the Indians gathered natural pigments from the earth and from plants. There is a Northern Plains Indian legend that says that the person searching for black pigment must not speak a word or it will disappear.

As usual, it's a good idea to practice with acrylic leather paint on scrap before painting your moccasin pieces, to see how the paint goes on and to make sure that it will stay on reasonably well. Let the trial scrap dry thoroughly—at least eight hours—and then test it (rub it gently, bend it).

The painted design can be done by itself or after outlining areas with the electric pen. In either case, transfer the design to the leather first, as described above. If the paint doesn't seem to cover the leather thickly enough,

you can let it dry for half an hour or so and go over the design again with more paint. Let the painted piece dry overnight before sewing.

Leather paint has an acrylic sealer in it, so it's not necessary to put anything over the painted surface. In fact, products that are sold as sealers for dye might remove the paint, so don't apply anything without testing it first on scrap. (The finished moccasin with this design is shown on page 117.)

BEADS

Here are three ways to decorate moccasins with beads: the lazy stitch, the overlay stitch, and edge beading. Although either the lazy stitch or the overlay stitch can be used for any design, the overlay stitch is better for designs involving long lines or curves, because the line of beads need not be broken by stitches. The lazy stitch works better with side-by-side rows or rays, since it's easier to work with just one needle for short stitches. Edge beading goes only on the edges of leather.

For all three kinds of beading, use a #7 glover's needle and regular sewing thread. Pull the thread over a piece of wax to help keep it from tangling. Guidelines can be lightly drawn on the leather with a pencil. When the beading is finished, put a drop of glue on each knot in the thread.

LAZY STITCH

The "lazy" stitch is probably called that because several beads are attached with only one stitch. Take a small stitch in the leather where it will

Blackfoot beaded legging moccasins.

be covered with beads and tie a square knot on the back side of the leather to secure the end. Put the needle through to the front (a) and string on several beads—no more than five. Arrange them where you want them, and push the needle to the back side (b). Repeat, building up the pattern with rows, rays, or spirals of beads. Pull each stitch snug but not so tight that the beading looks puckered. Take another hidden stitch or two at the end, and tie the thread to itself on the back side.

a

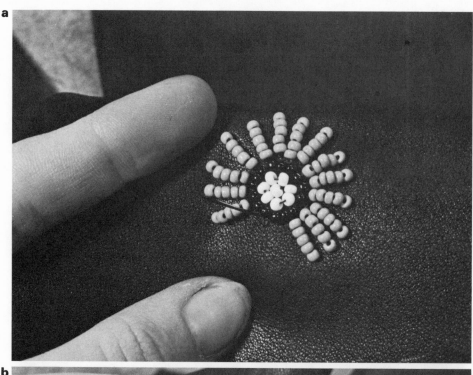

b

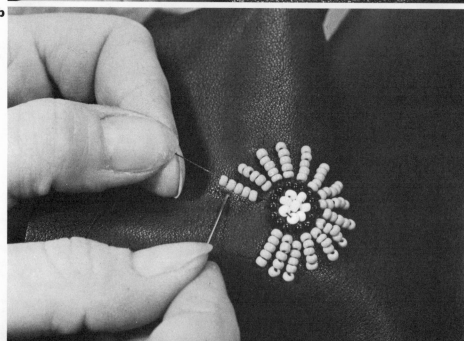

OVERLAY STITCH

For the overlay stitch you need two #7 glover's needles. Put one on each end of the thread. Push one needle through to the back side of the leather, leaving about half of the thread on each side. String some beads on the top thread and arrange them the way you want them (a). Pick up the needle on the back side and bring it through the leather on one side of the row of beads, three or four beads from the beginning (b). Cross to the opposite side of the bead row and put the needle through to the back side (c). Repeat, holding the bead row in place with stitches every few beads. Pull the stitches snug as you go. At the end of the design, put both needles to the back side and tie the threads in a square knot.

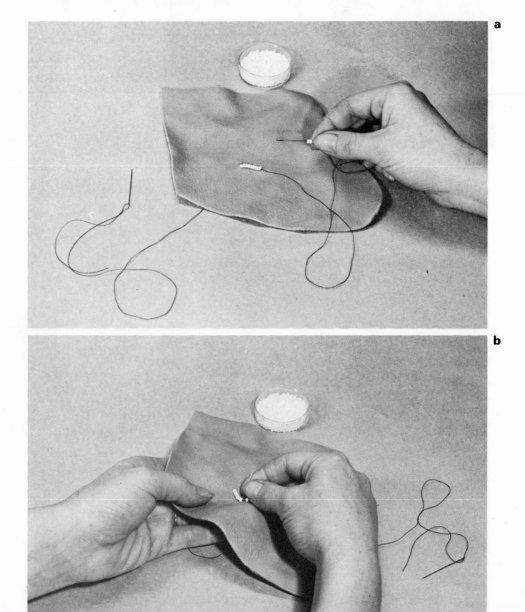

a

b

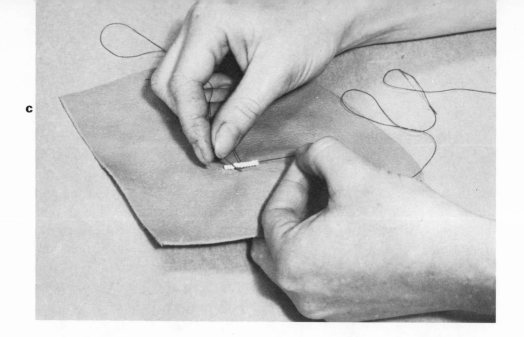

c

It is a good idea to cover the back side of a beaded area by gluing on a layer of thin leather or felt. This is not essential, but it prevents the knots from possibly irritating the foot and helps to keep threads and knots from coming undone.

EDGE BEADING

Edge beading is a traditional form of decoration on Eastern Woodland Indian moccasins, such as the Seneca (New York) moccasin in the photo. The beads can be all of one color, or they can be of alternating colors.

Seneca moccasins with edge beading.

42

If the leather might need to be trimmed, the beading should be done after the moccasin is sewn together. For example, the edge of a cuff ends with a heel seam, which often must be trimmed; in this case the beading should be done after the heel seam is finished.

Put the needle through the leather about ⅛″ from the edge. Tie a square knot over the edge of the leather (a) to secure the thread end. Put on one bead, and put the needle through the leather again (b). The distance between stitches should be a little more than the width of one bead—for seed beads, the stitches are ⅛″ apart. Pass the needle up through the bead (c). Put on two beads and take another stitch through the leather (d). If you are using two colors, the bead of the second color goes on the needle first. Pass the needle up through the second bead (e). Repeat, putting on

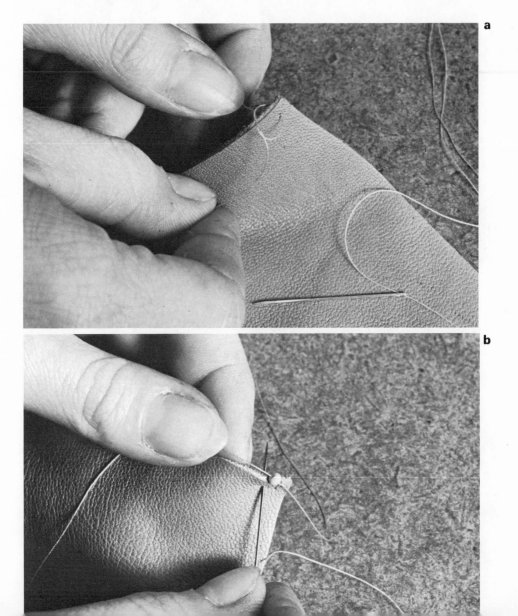

a

b

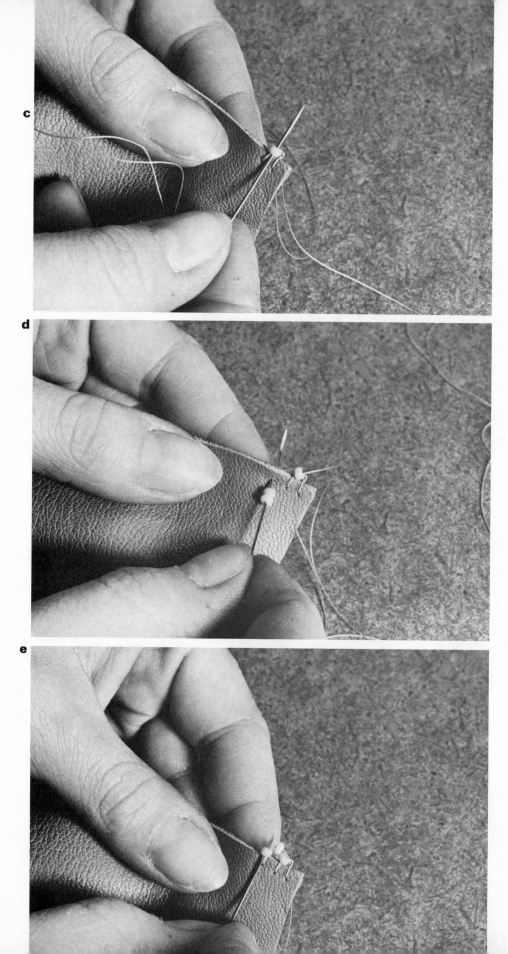

two more beads and taking a stitch, then passing the needle up through the second bead. The first bead is the only one that goes on by itself; after that, always put on two at a time.

At the end of the beading, take a stitch through the leather and tie a square knot over the edge. A drop of glue helps to keep the knots tied.

There are many other ways of decorating with beads. The book list mentions several of the many books available on beading designs and techniques.

SEWING

When the decorations (if any) are in place, the pieces are ready to be sewn together. All of the styles in this book except Penobscot are sewn with glover's needle and whipstitch, and the instructions for this method follow. For Penobscot, see the instructions below for harness needles and double cross-stitch.

Don't forget to keep checking the moccasins for fit as you go. Each time you make a seam, try them on before starting to sew. You will need a ⅛″ margin on each piece for the seam; if the pieces are too large, trim away the excess before sewing. It is unlikely that the pieces will be too small. Keep in mind that the leather will stretch somewhat as you wear it. Also, it is easy to stretch a piece slightly to make it fit as you sew it to another piece. Just pull it a *very* small amout on each stitch. If by some chance a piece is much too small and you're positive it won't work, you can either cut a new larger piece or sew in an additional piece.

Before sewing two pieces of soft leather together, it is sometimes helpful to staple the seam with a paper stapler to hold it in place. This also helps with the fitting. Stapling is not essential; try sewing with and without it to see which works best for you. I prefer to staple long seams and curved seams, which tend to pull out of shape more than short straight ones. To staple a seam, staple the two ends of the seam first, then the middle, then fill in with staples all along the seam. When the seam is finished, the staples can be removed with a staple remover or screwdriver.

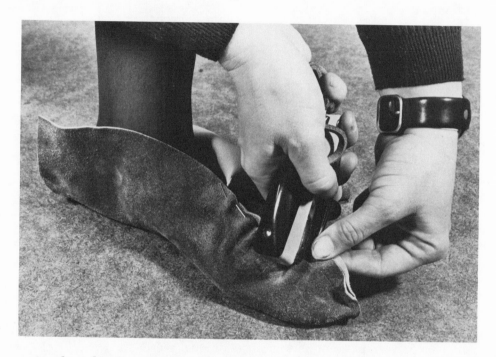

Stapling does not work on the heavier retanned leather, but you'll find it unnecessary anyway, for the molded sole does not stretch out of shape the way soft leather does. When joining a soft leather piece to a retanned sole, keep checking to make sure that the seam is not pulled out of shape. You may need to stretch or gather very small amounts to make the ends come out even. (In some cases, you needn't worry about the ends coming out even, because the excess leather will be trimmed off.)

When the moccasin is to be turned right side out after sewing, place the right sides together, with the wrong or "in" sides showing. If it is not to be turned after sewing, place the wrong sides together and sew with the right sides out.

Cut a piece of thread approximately six times as long as the seam. If you are doing a very short seam, like a 2″ heel seam, it's better to add some extra thread to the 12″ for convenience. The glover's needle has a large eye and should be easy to thread. Cut a square, clean end on the thread and pinch the end flat with your fingers to make it slide into the eye.

In some cases, you'll be starting to sew in the middle of a seam. If so, draw the thread through to half of its length on the first stitch, leaving half for the other part of the seam. If you are starting at the end of a seam, the thread end will need to be secured. Sometimes there is or will be another thread near the end of the seam, and you can tie the thread ends together in a square knot. Leave a long tail on the thread end for this purpose. If there will be no other thread end to tie to, put the needle through the leather once and tie the thread end to the rest of the thread, over the edge of the leather, in a square knot.

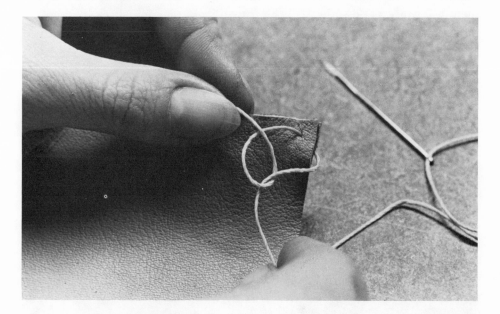

The glover's needle has a sharp triangular point. When pushing or pulling it, hold it by the rounded part behind the sharp edges, never by the edges themselves. To make sure that the needle doesn't slip and slice your fingers if it is difficult to push through the leather, try pushing it against your work surface until it is through the leather far enough to grasp easily.

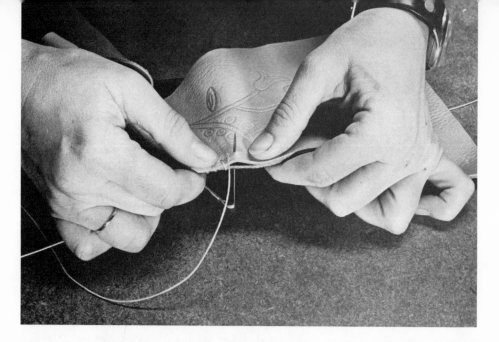

For the whipstitch, the needle goes through both layers about ⅛″ from the edge. It goes around the edge, then comes up through the leather again, making a loop or spiral around the edges. Make the stitches close together for looks and strength—between ¹⁄₁₆″ and ⅛″ apart—and space them as evenly as possible. Pull the thread snug on each stitch, but not so tight that it puckers up the seam. Keep checking as you sew to make sure

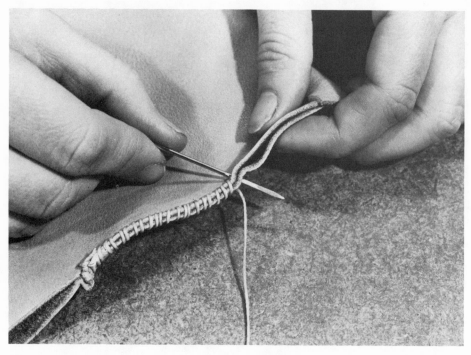

that you are not pulling the layers unevenly. If, however, it looks as though you won't have enough of the top piece to fit onto the sole, for example, you can stretch the top piece a little bit to fit.

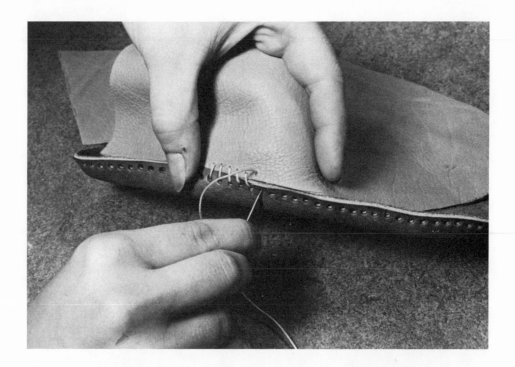

At the seam end, put the needle through to the back side of the leather. Wherever possible, tie thread ends together in a tight square knot. Where there is only one thread end and no other thread nearby to tie to, sew back along the seam for a few stitches, being careful not to cut the thread with the sharp point of the needle, and tie the thread end to one of the stitches. Put a drop of rubber cement on each knot and let it dry thoroughly (about 20 minutes).

DOUBLE CROSS-STITCH

This stitch, used in the Penobscot style, is sewed with dull harness needles instead of sharp glover's needles, because the holes are punched in both layers of leather before sewing. Also, the sharp point of the glover's needle might cut the thread when it goes through the hole a second time.

Cut the thread twelve times the seam length. Place the two leather pieces side by side, not overlapping. Put a harness needle on each end of the thread and sew up through the first hole of each piece from the bottom; pull up the thread until the ends are even. Then, with one needle, cross over to the other side and go into the second hole. With the other needle, cross over and go into the second hole on that side (a). Make the thread cross, on the back, to its original side, and come out the *second* holes (b).

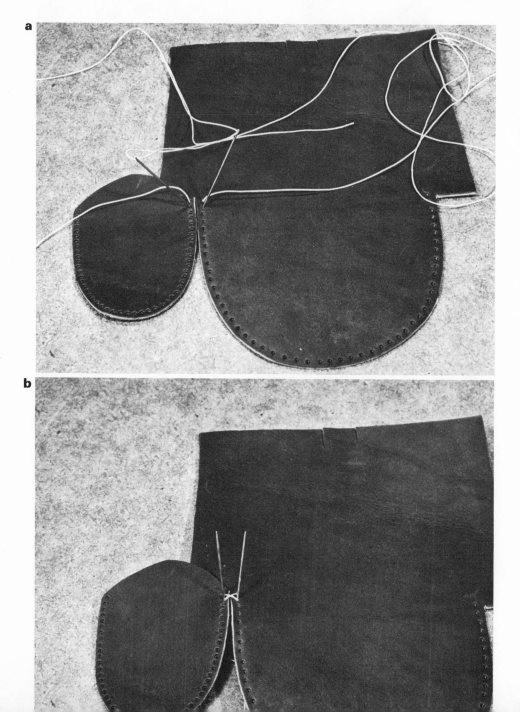

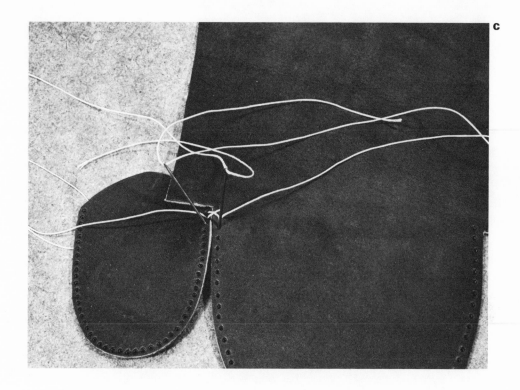

Cross over on the top again, and put the needles in the third holes (c). Cross over on the back again and come out the third holes. Continue in this way. Note that the threads make an X on the top side but not on the back side; on the back side they go straight across. Except for the first holes, the thread goes through each hole twice.

Pull the thread tight on each stitch. When two different-sized curved pieces are being sewn together, as in the Penobscot toe, it is necessary to pull quite firmly at each stitch in order to gather the larger curve up to fit the smaller one. It's easier to do this if you hold the two pieces so that the holes are lined up opposite each other as much as possible before putting in the needle.

At the seam end, sew backwards for a stitch or two, put the needles through to the back side of the leather, and tie a square knot. Put a dab of rubber cement on the knot.

Whether you use the whipstitch or the double cross-stitch, it's a good idea to tap your seams flat after sewing. When the glue is dry, put the seam

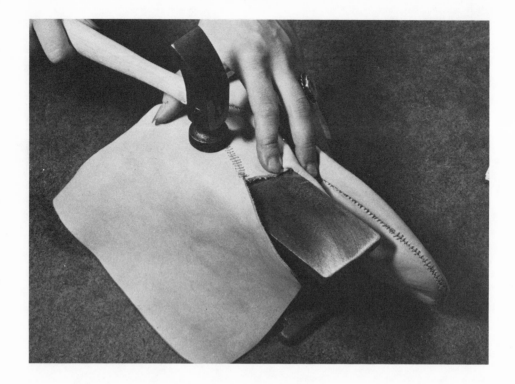

on the anvil and tap the stitching and knots flat with the hammer. Flatter seams and knots are more comfortable where they touch the foot; they look neater; and knots that have been tapped flat are less likely to come undone. (Some seams are impossible to reach with hammer and anvil, and they cannot be tapped flat.)

BOTTOM SOLES

The final step for many moccasins is to glue on the flat bottom soles of rubber. The reasons for adding these soles have been mentioned on page 15; if you would rather not put them on, consider adding a layer of leather instead. The additional layer (rubber or leather) will cover and protect any stitching, and when the sole begins to wear out, you can replace it easily, without having to remake the entire moccasin.

Put the moccasin on your foot, place it on the soling material, and draw around it with a pencil. Make sure that you have the correct side of the soling material up, if there is a difference. Draw the outline just around the part of the moccasin touching the soling material as you stand on it. Don't try to make the sole larger than the flat part and glue it up the curved sides, because the glue isn't strong enough to hold that way.

Cut out the foot shape with shears or a razor cutter. You can either cut out the exact shape right on the line, or leave a margin outside the line, glue on the sole, and then trim it.

If you will be gluing the rubber to a smooth leather surface (molded soles, for example), rough up the grain of the leather with sandpaper or a file so that the glue will hold better. Sometimes galosh soling has a slightly greasy feel on the side you will be gluing to the moccasin. The glue will stick better if you wipe the surface clean with a little lacquer thinner on a rag.

Spread a thin, even coat of glue on both of the surfaces that are to be bonded together. Take care to spread the glue all the way out to the edges. Glue is difficult if not impossible to remove, so try not to let any drip on the wrong places! If it does, let it dry thoroughly, then try rubbing it off with your fingers or a rubber eraser. Sometimes glue can be lightly sanded off with fine sandpaper.

If there are any thread knots near the glued area, press them into the glue with your finger so that the knots will be hidden under the sole.

Contact cement needs to dry *before* the pieces are put together. Set the pieces, glued sides up, in the sun if possible, and wait until the glue is "tacky" (not entirely dry, but not so wet that it comes off on the fingers easily). This usually takes 20 to 30 minutes. The warmth of direct sunlight makes the glue stick better, but it is not absolutely essential. It's also possible to put the moccasins and soles near the radiator or heater; this works well, but take care—rubber cement is highly flammable, and it must be kept away from flames and heating coils. Also, be sure that the pieces don't get too hot.

It's not necessary to return to the pieces in *exactly* 20 minutes. They can wait for an hour or so if necessary. Sometimes, with very dry leather, the glue seems to soak in and feel entirely dry; if that happens, apply another coat of glue and wait again.

When the glue is ready, put the pieces together, aligning them carefully, since it is difficult to pull them apart again. Trim the soles if they need it. Squeeze the whole cemented area together with your fingers, especially at the edges, or, if possible, put the moccasins on the anvil and tap the glued pieces together with the hammer.

PRESERVING, CLEANING, REPAIRS

PRESERVING

Retanned cowhide soles need oil once in a while so they don't dry out and crack. It's not necessary to oil them right away when they are new, but do it after a month or so of wear, and every month or so after that. Good oils for the job are silicone shoe oil (smells terrible but works well), neat's-foot oil, mink oil, and Lexol (a brand of neat's-foot oil combined with silicone oil and other goodies). Saddle soap is not oil; it is a cleaner.

Oil sometimes darkens the leather. This is usually temporary, but occasionally the leather stays a little darker. Try the oil on scrap first if this matters to you.

These oils will also help to make the moccasins water-resistant—that is, water will run off rather than soaking in as much as it would on unoiled leather—but you cannot make leather completely waterproof without doing something like covering it in plastic. One of the fine things about leather is that it "breathes"—allows air and moisture to pass through. This makes moccasins comfortable to wear, so you wouldn't want to seal the leather up. If the moccasins are wet from washing or rain, set them to dry where air can circulate around them, and *away* from direct sun or heat (water plus heat stiffens and dries the leather out too much). Don't put them in the dryer! Remember that moccasins will need oil eventually if they get drenched very often.

CLEANING

Always try out any cleaning technique on scrap before using it on your moccasins. Small stains can sometimes be removed by erasing with a clean rubber eraser or by lightly sanding with sandpaper. Often, dirt and stains can be sponged off with warm water and mild soap. The moccasins can be washed with mild soap, too—but results vary a lot. Some leathers and suedes look fine after being washed gently, by hand; sometimes they come out stiffer, or the color changes. Suede is usually "gummed down" somewhat by washing. Suede spray or mink-oil spray (available from leather-supply stores and shoe-repair shops) may replace the oils removed by washing and restore softness; try them out on scrap first. Dry-cleaning fluids may remove the color from the surrounding area as well as the stain, so I don't recommend their use.

REPAIRS

Your moccasins should last a long time—many years—if they have been made with good-quality materials and reasonable care. Usually the first thing that wears out is the sole. If you have used a flat sole layer of rubber or leather, it's very easy to pull off the old sole and replace it. If the glue sticks *too* well, making it hard to remove the sole, you can use lacquer thinner or Barge cement thinner to help get the soles off. Put on a couple of drops at a time as you pull away the old sole.

If a hole develops in the upper part, you can patch it by gluing on a piece that is a little bigger than the hole and whipstitching it in place. If the leather is torn but all the pieces are still there, it can sometimes be mended invisibly by gluing a small patch on the inside and carefully laying down the torn parts to match up exactly. The patch may not stay without any stitching, but it's worth a try.

After a period of time or with rough wear, glued soles may start to come off (especially if they weren't well stuck to begin with). Just pull the sole back a little more and reglue it. Make sure that it is flat and trim it if it's not, since it's too much to expect of the glue to hold the sole up on the curve of the foot. While the glue is getting tacky, the partially removed sole can be propped away from the moccasin with a toothpick or something like that.

Eastern Woodland Type Moccasins

SHAWNEE

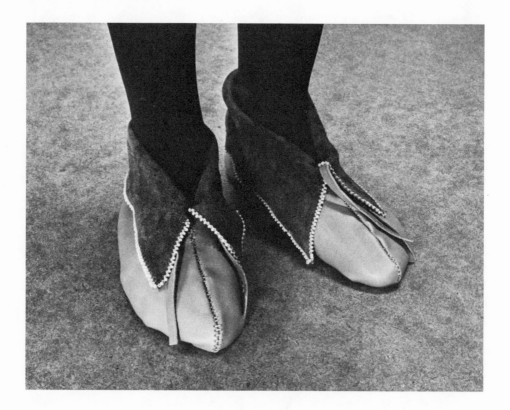

Materials: Soft leather, thread, about 4 feet of thong (optional), sponge (optional), leather and glue for bottom soles (optional)

Tools: Cutter, stapler, glover's needle, punch for thong holes (optional)

1. Draw a foot outline in the middle of a large piece of paper; the paper should be at least 2 feet square. Draw a heel-toe line in the middle of the foot (see page 25).

2. Measure to find the halfway point along this line. Now measure ¾" closer to the toe end and make a mark there.

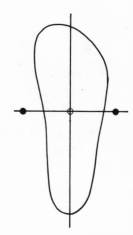

3. Measure all the way around your arch at the mark you made (see page 23). Write down the measurement.

Divide the measurement in half and add ¼". Draw a line perpendicular (crosswise) to the heel-toe line through the mark you made in step 2 and center the halved measurement on the line.

4. Measure out from the toe and heel along the heel-toe line and mark two points: ⅜″ to ½″ out is good for fairly snug moccasins; go out a bit more if you want them floppy.

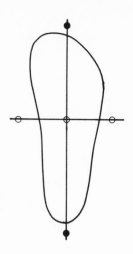

5. At the mark you made on the inside of the foot in step 3, draw a line parallel to the heel-toe line. Mark a point on this line about where your big toe joins your foot—this is not an exact point!

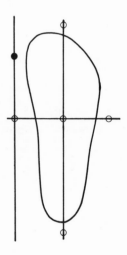

6. Now you can draw the curve, as shown, from the point you just marked around to the mark on the outside of the foot. Go through the toe point you marked in step 4. Put in a line perpendicular to the heel-toe line at the heel point you marked in step 4.

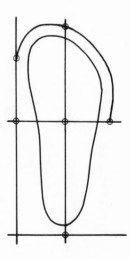

7. Now for the cuffs. Mark a point on the line you drew in step 3 about 1″ to 3″ past the mark on the outside of the foot. Make it near if you want small cuffs, 3″ or more away if you want big ones—you can always trim them!

Draw a line through this new point parallel to the heel-toe line. Now draw the angled line, as shown, for the cuff points. The angled line shouldn't extend past the toe, or you'll be tripping on the cuffs—but if you find they are too long, you can trim them.

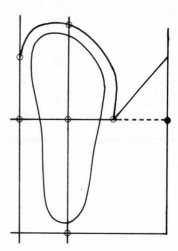

8. Fold the paper double along the left-hand line (I *told* you to use a big piece!). Cut out the pattern. Do *not* cut along the left-hand (fold) line.

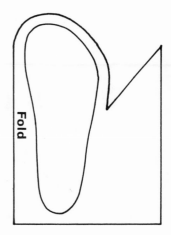

9. At the heel end, cut a little snip (½″ long) on each side of the fold line about ½″ to ⅝″ away from the line.

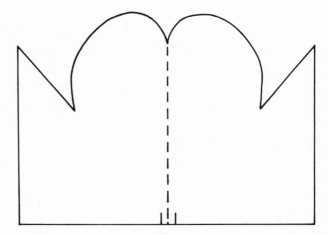

CONSTRUCTION

1. Cut two of the pattern from leather—right and left are the same.

2. Fold the leather along the middle (fold) line, wrong side out. Staple the seam (⅛″ from the edge) from the fold to the end of the curve. Put your foot in the moccasin to check the fit. If it is too loose, put in more staples to make it fit snugly. Take off the moccasin and trim the curve if necessary to ⅛″ outside the line of staples. Pull out the staples.

3. Decorate as desired. If you are going to decorate the cuffs, remember to put the decorations on the inside of the leather so that they will show when the cuffs are turned down on the finished moccasins.

4. Fold the leather along the fold line again, wrong side out. Sew (whipstitch) from the fold to the end of the curve.

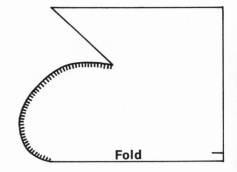

5. Turn the moccasin right side out and turn down the cuffs. Put your foot in, and hold the heel edges together to check the fit. Remember that the leather will stretch some as you wear it. Trim off at the heel if necessary, leaving ⅛″ for the seam. Turn the moccasin wrong side out again and sew up the back seam, leaving the space between the heel cuts free at the bottom.

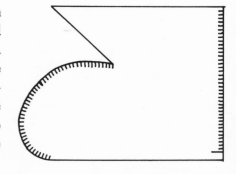

6. The space between the heel cuts forms the heel tab. Leaving the moccasin turned wrong side out, tuck in the heel tab so that it will show when the moccasin is turned right side out. Sew across the heel. Turn the moccasin right side out, turn down the cuffs, and cut the heel tab into a decorative shape if you like.

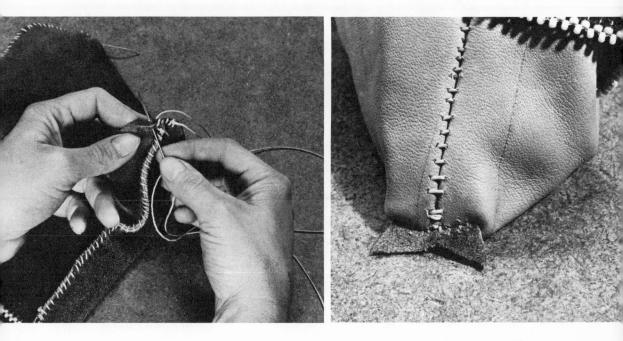

If the moccasins seem too floppy, you can punch an even number of holes, spaced about 1″ apart, just below the fold line of the cuff and add a tie thong to help keep the moccasins on your feet.

7. *Sponge insole* (optional): Outline the foot on sponge, cut it out, and slip the insole into the moccasin.

8. *Bottom sole* (optional): Following the directions on page 52, cut out and glue on a leather bottom sole (this moccasin is too soft for a rubber bottom sole).

WINNEBAGO

Materials: Soft leather, thread, sponge (optional), leather and glue for bottom soles (optional)

Tools: Cutter, stapler, glover's needle

THE PATTERN

1. Draw a foot outline. Draw a heel-toe line in the middle of the foot (see page 25).

2. Mark points on the heel-toe line ½″ out from the toe and ¾″ out from the heel. Draw a line perpendicular to the heel-toe line at the heel point.

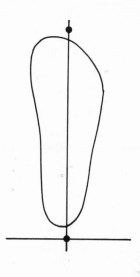

3. Put your foot on the foot outline. Lift your heel slightly and mark a point on the heel-toe line that corresponds to the highest point of your arch. Take away your foot and draw a line perpendicular to the heel-toe line at that point.

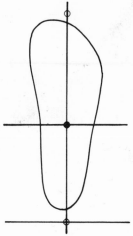

4. Put your foot back on the foot outline and measure all the way around the arch at the point you marked in step 3. Divide the measurement in half. Center the halved measurement on the line you drew in step 3.

5. Measure to find the point halfway between the point you marked in step 3 and the toe end of the foot outline. Draw a line perpendicular to the heel-toe line at this point. Repeat step 4 at this new point, measuring the arch at the new point and centering the halved measurement on the new line.

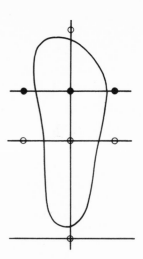

6. Draw a curve from the inside to the outside of the foot. Start about where your big toe joins your foot, connect the points you made in steps 4 and 5, and then draw straight down to the heel line, as shown.

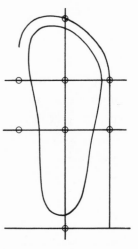

7. Now start where your curve starts at the inside of your foot and draw a straight line to the heel line on that side.

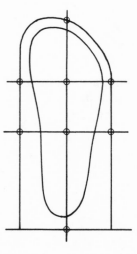

8. Fold the paper on the line you drew in step 7 and cut out the pattern. Do not cut on the fold.

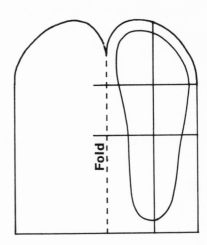

9. Place the pattern on a large piece of paper and draw around it, allowing room to add the cuff. Fold the original pattern and transfer the fold line. On the new pattern, draw lines for heel cuts on either side of the fold line; make them ¾″ long and ⅜″ away from the fold line.

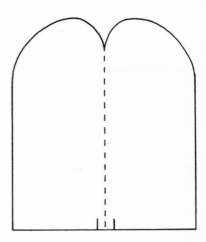

10. Add the cuff: Draw a guideline across the toes, and another line 1″ in front of that and parallel to it.

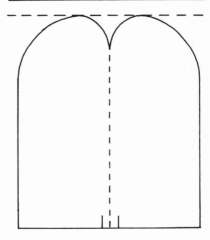

11. Measure the total distance from the heel line to the front line along one side. Divide this measurement in half, and mark the halfway point.

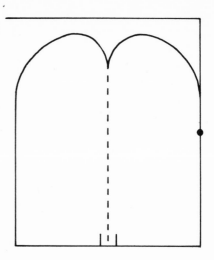

12. On the same side, measure 3″ out along the front line and mark a point there. Extend the heel line in the same direction and mark the 3″ point.

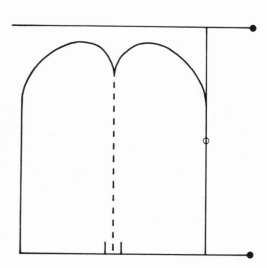

13. Measure the length of your foot outline along the heel-toe line and draw a perpendicular line half that length out from the point you marked in step **11.**

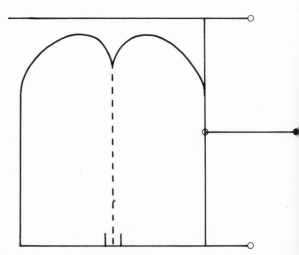

14. Measure the widest part of the foot outline and subtract ½″. Draw a line this length perpendicular to the line you drew in step 13, at the far end of this line and centered on it. Connect this new line to the 3″ lines at front and heel. Whew! All that for a cuff!

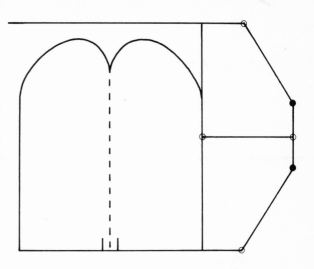

15. Cut out the paper pattern.

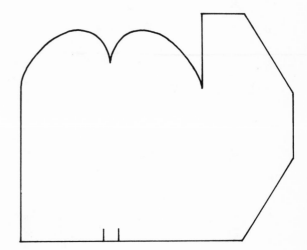

CONSTRUCTION

1. Cut a right and a left of the one pattern piece from leather.

2. Fold the leather on the fold line, wrong side out. Staple the seam (⅛″ from the edge) from the fold to the cuff fold line. Put your foot in the moccasin to check the fit. If it is too loose, put in more staples to make it fit snugly. Take off the moccasin and trim the curve if necessary to ⅛″ outside the line of staples. Pull out the staples.

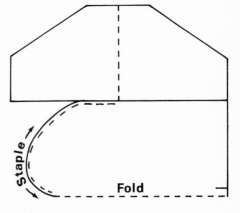

3. Decorate as desired. If you are going to decorate the cuffs, remember to put the decorations on the inside of the leather so that they will show when the cuffs are turned down on the finished moccasins.

4. Fold the leather on the fold line again, wrong side out, and sew (whipstitch) from the fold to the cuff fold line.

5. Fold the cuff in half, right sides in, and whipstitch the bottom of the cuff to the top of the sole.

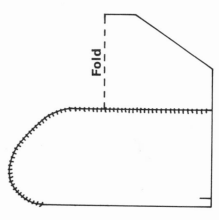

6. Sew up the heel seam, starting above the heel cuts and stopping where the cuff starts.

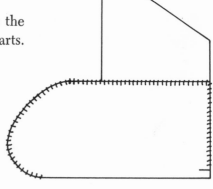

7. The space between the heel cuts forms the heel tab. Leaving the moccasin turned wrong side out, tuck in the heel tab so that it will show when the moccasin is turned right side out. Sew across the heel. Turn the moccasin right side out, turn down the cuff, and cut the heel tab into a decorative shape if you like (see page 61).

8. *Sponge insole* (optional): Outline the foot on sponge, cut it out, and slip the insole into the moccasin.

9. *Bottom sole* (optional): Following the directions on page 52, cut out and glue on a leather bottom sole (this moccasin is too soft for a rubber bottom sole).

PENOBSCOT

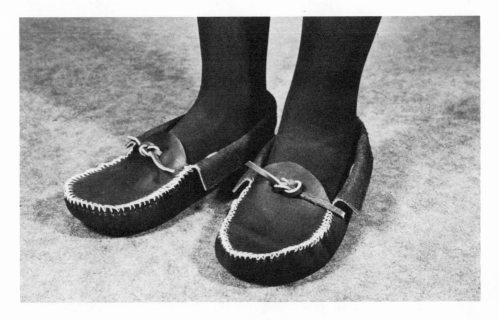

Materials: Retanned cowhide (up to 6-ounce) or soft leather, thread, about 4 feet of retanned thong, sponge (optional), rubber or leather and glue for bottom soles (optional).

69

Tools: 6-to-the-inch stitchmarker, ruler, cutter, #oo punch, two #ooo harness needles, larger punch for thong holes (optional)

THE PATTERN

1. *Main piece:* Draw a foot outline. Draw a heel-toe line in the middle of the foot (see page 25).

2. On the heel-toe line, mark a point 1¼" out from the toe. Mark a point ¾" out from the heel, and draw a line perpendicular to the heel-toe line at this point.

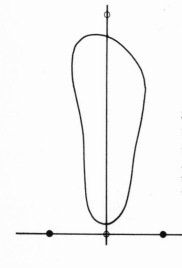

3. To determine the height of the moccasin, measure up the back of your foot from the floor to the top of the heel; mine is 3". Add ½". Mark points on the perpendicular line this distance out from the heel-toe line on both sides.

4. Mark a point on the heel-toe line halfway between toe and heel of the foot outline. Mark another point ¾″ closer to the toe end and draw a line perpendicular to the heel-toe line there. Mark points as in step 3 on this new line.

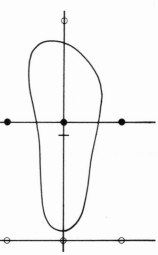

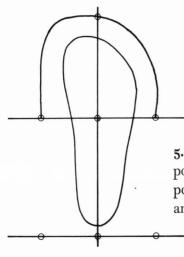

5. Draw a curve around the toe end, connecting the points you made in step 4 and going through the point you marked in step 2. The curve should be fat and rounded, not pointed.

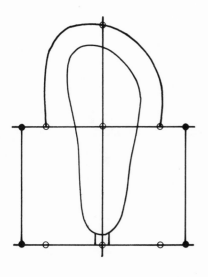

6. For cuffs, measure out 1″ on each side from the points you marked in steps 3 and 4. Draw lines connecting these new points. Draw two heel cuts, each one ⅜″ from the heel-toe line and ¾″ long.

7. Cut out the paper pattern.

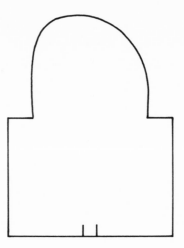

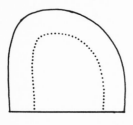

8. *Vamp:* Draw around the rounded toe-curve portion of the main-piece pattern. Draw a straight line connecting the ends of the curve.

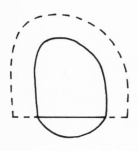

9. Measure and mark many points 1½″ in from the outer edge and connect the dots in a smooth curve.

10. Draw a shape you like for the tongue. This will be the edge of the vamp pattern. Mine is a smooth curve extending 1″ out from the midpoint of the straight edge.

11. Cut out the vamp pattern.

12. *Sewing holes:* Mark the position of sewing holes on the toe-curve portion of the vamp pattern with a 6-to-the-inch stitchmarker, ⅛″ from the edge. Mark the points with a pencil so they can be seen easily.

13. Mark sewing hole positions on the toe-curve portion of the main-piece pattern using a ruler—make them ¼″ apart and ⅛″ from the edge.

14. Count the marks. There should be the same number of holes on the vamp as on the main piece. If the numbers don't match, change the spacing of the main-piece holes slightly, adding or subtracting hole marks as needed. Recheck to make sure that the number of holes is the same on vamp and main piece.

CONSTRUCTION

1. Cut a right and a left of the vamp and main piece from leather. Cut the heel cuts.

2. To mark sewing holes on vamp and main piece, hold the paper pattern on the leather and press a pencil point on each dot to mark through to the leather. Punch the holes with a #00 punch.

3. Decorate as desired. If you are going to decorate the cuffs, remember to put the decorations on the inside of the leather so that they will show when the cuffs are turned down on the finished moccasins.

4. Sew the vamp to the main piece: Cut a piece of thread twelve times the seam length and put a harness needle on each end of the thread. Put one needle through the first vamp hole from the back to the front side, and the other needle through the first main-piece hole from the back to the front side (see page 50). Using double cross-stitch (page 49), sew the seam, gathering up the main piece to fit the vamp. Tie the thread ends in a square knot.

5. Try on the moccasin. If there is an overlap at the back, trim the back seam evenly so that the edges just meet.

6. With the stitchmarker, mark hole spacing ⅛″ in from the two heel edges. Do not mark holes on the heel tab (between the heel cuts). Now punch #oo holes at the marks. Sew the heel seam with double cross-stitch, starting at the top. Don't tie off the thread ends yet.

7. Punch four #oo holes near the corners of the heel tab. Fold up the heel tab and mark through it for the matching holes underneath. Punch these holes, inserting the punch through the heel tab opening. With the threaded needles from step 6, sew up the tab, going through the holes two or three times; then tie the thread ends in a square knot on the inside.

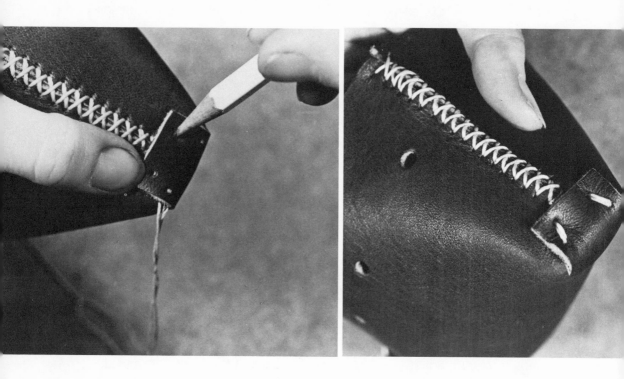

8. Measure and mark thong holes—two in the tongue, and an odd number along each side, with the last hole near the end of the cuff. The holes should be just below the fold line of the cuff—about 1¼″ from the edge— and spaced about 1″ apart. Punch the holes. Starting at the tongue, put in the thong, weaving it in and out, and tie the ends in a square knot. Turn down the cuff. If necessary to make the cuff stay down, tap the fold with a hammer.

74

9. *Sponge insole* (optional): Outline the foot on sponge, cut it out, and slip the insole into the moccasin.

10. *Bottom sole* (optional): Following the directions on page 52, cut out and glue on a rubber or leather bottom sole.

SOFT, EDGE-BEADED VARIATION

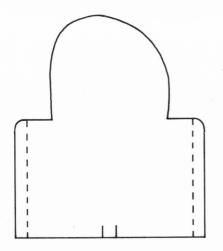

To make a pair like these, use the Penobscot pattern. In step 6, measure out 1½″ for the cuff instead of 1″. Make rounded corners on the cuffs. Use soft leather for vamp and main piece. Edge-bead the cuff and tongue. Sew the moccasins together using the suede side out on the vamp and the top-grain (smooth) side out on the main piece, so that the sueded side of the cuffs will show when the moccasins are finished. Omit the tie thongs.

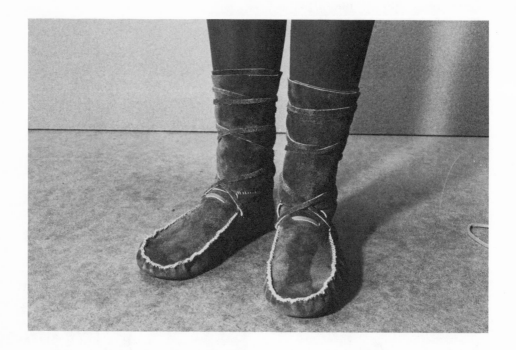

Make the Penobscot pattern through step 3. In step 4, instead of marking a point ¾″ closer to the toe end, mark the point ¾″ closer to the heel end. Draw a longer tongue (step 10), making it extend 2″ out from the midpoint of the straight edge instead of 1″.

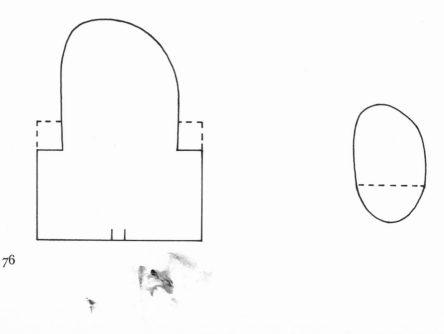

Make a leg-piece pattern—a rectangle 6″ high and as long as the distance around the foot outline (the perimeter). Cut out the three pattern pieces and mark sewing holes in the main piece and the toe-curve portion of the vamp (steps 12 to 14).

Since the vamp of this pattern extends farther up on the foot, you may have to make the vamp wider. Put your foot on the main-piece pattern and measure all the way around your arch at the point where the sewing holes start. Measure across the vamp from first sewing hole to last sewing hole. Measure across the main piece from first sewing hole to last sewing hole. Add these two pattern measurements. If the total is less than your arch measurement, widen the vamp the necessary amount, as the diagram

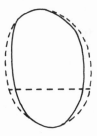

shows, by drawing around it on another piece of paper. Mark sewing holes on the new edges.

Construct the moccasin through step 7. Use soft leather for all pieces. Sew on the leg piece following directions for Flathead (page 102). Punch two thong holes in the tongue and one on each side of the main piece near the corner where the cuff starts. Use about 5 feet of thong; thread the thong ends into the tongue holes and out the main-piece holes. Wrap the thong around the leg piece and tie the ends in a square knot.

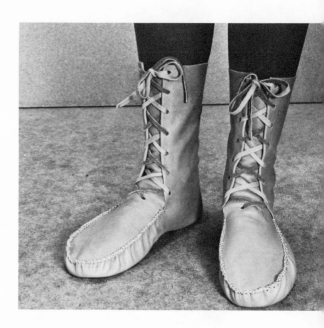

Make the Penobscot pattern through step 3. In step 4, instead of marking a point ¾″ closer to the toe end, mark the point ¾″ closer to the heel end. Draw a longer tongue (step 10), making it extend 7″ out from the mid-point of the straight edge instead of 1″.

On the main-piece pattern, extend the cuff 6 inches to each side to make the leg piece. Add ½″ to the front edge of the extension. Cut out the two pattern pieces and mark sewing holes in the main piece and the toe-curve portion of the vamp (steps 12 to 14).

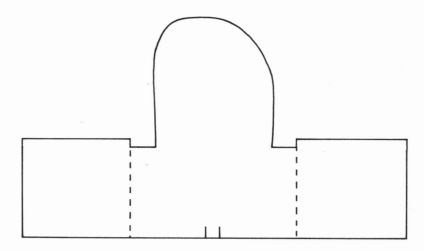

Since the vamp of this pattern extends farther up on the foot, you may have to make the vamp wider. Put your foot on the main-piece pattern and measure all the way around your arch at the point where the sewing holes start. Measure across the vamp from first sewing hole to last sewing hole. Measure across the main piece from first sewing hole to last sewing hole. Add these two pattern measurements. If the total is less than your arch measurement, widen the vamp the necessary amount, as the diagram shows, by drawing around it on another piece of paper. Mark sewing holes on the new edges.

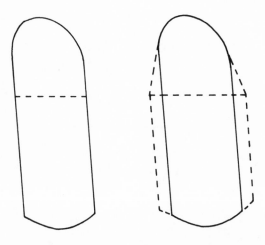

Construct the moccasin through step 7. Use soft leather for vamp and main piece. In step 5, fit the entire back seam by stapling the back edges together ⅛″ from the edge, trying on the moccasin, and putting in more staples if necessary to make a snug fit. Trim if necessary to within ⅛″ of the staples. Remove staples after sewing.

On the front edges of the leg piece, turn the ½″ extension to the inside and glue it down. Punch two thong holes on the tongue and six or seven on each front edge, spaced about 1″ apart and ¼″ from the edge. Use about 5 feet of thong; thread the thong ends out the tongue holes and then lace up the front.

Plains Type Moccasins

SHOSHONE

Materials: Retanned cowhide for soles, soft leather for tops, thread, about 5 feet of thong, rubber or leather and glue for bottom soles, sponge (optional)

Tools: Cutter, stitchmarker (optional), #oo punch, glover's needle, larger punch for thong holes (optional)

1. *Sole:* Draw a foot outline. Draw a line ¼″ out from the outline all the way around and cut the pattern out.

2. *Top:* Draw another foot outline. Draw a heel-toe line in the middle of the foot (see page 25).

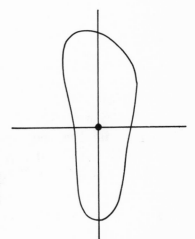

3. Mark the halfway point between heel and toe, and draw a line perpendicular to the heel-toe line at that point.

4. Measure all the way around the arch at the point you marked in step 3 (see page 23). Write down the measurement.

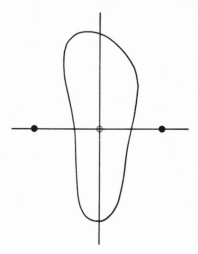

5. Measure the width of the foot outline at the midline you drew in step 3 and subtract this measurement from the arch measurement (step 4). Add ½″ and center the resulting measurement on the midline.

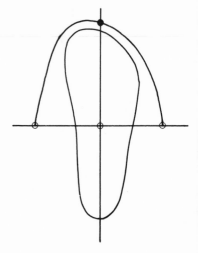

6. Mark a point on the heel-toe line ½″ out from the toe. Now draw a curve connecting this point with the ones you marked in step 5.

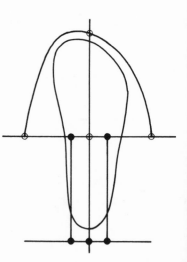

7. Next—the tongue: Mark two points on the midline, each 1″ from the heel-toe line. Measure ¾″ out from the heel and draw a line perpendicular to the heel-toe line at that point. Mark two points on this new line, each 1″ from the heel-toe line. Connect these points with the points you just marked on the midline to make the lines for the tongue.

8. Add the fork: Mark a point on the heel-toe line for the center of the fork; you can make the fork any shape you want by choosing this point. Mine is ¾″ in from the heel end of the foot outline. Draw slanted lines to connect the center of the fork with the end of the tongue, as shown.

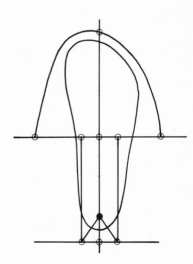

9. Now the heel: Measure from the floor up the back of your foot to where you want the moccasin to reach—probably between 3″ and 4″. Measure that distance out from the edge of the tongue on each side; mark points.

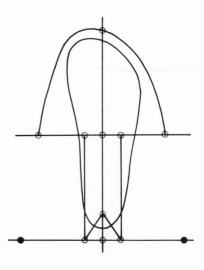

10. You want the heel to come in a little at the top of the moccasin, so it will stay on your foot—so mark points ½″ up from the tongue points and draw the slanted heel lines, as shown.

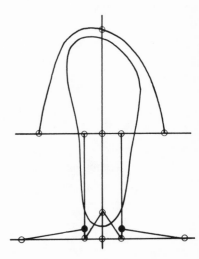

11. Continue the curve to connect the front and back. The ends of the curve meet the heel line at the points you marked in step 9.

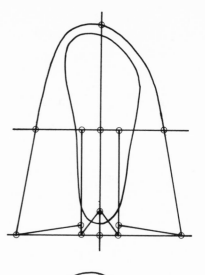

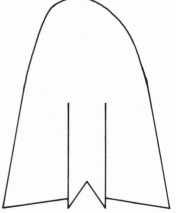

12. Cut out the paper pattern. Cut along the tongue lines.

CONSTRUCTION

1. Using the sole pattern, cut one right and one left of the retanned cowhide. Cut a right and a left top piece of the soft leather. Cut along the tongue lines.

2. Mark placement of sewing holes on the sole piece ⅛″ from the edge. Use a stitchmarker or a ruler; if you use a ruler, make the marks ³⁄₁₆″ apart. Punch #00 holes at the marked points.

3. Decorate the tops as desired. If you are going to decorate the tongues, remember to put the decorations on the inside of the leather so that they will show when the tongues are turned over on the finished moccasins.

84

4. Whipstitch the top piece to the sole piece: Place the inside of the top piece on the smooth side of the sole piece (the top-grain side of the sole is placed so that it will be next to the foot; the bottom sole will be glued to the rough side of the leather). Start sewing at the toe, whipstitch around to the heel, and then start again at the toe and sew the other side. Use one sole hole per stitch.

5. Try on the moccasin and hold the heel edges together to check the fit. Trim off at the heel edges if necessary, leaving ⅛″ for the seam. Starting at the bottom, sew up the heel seam, right sides out.

6. Mark the position of thong holes: Fold the tongue down over the top toward the toes, placing the fold where you want it—see the photograph for the way I fold mine. Mark two thong holes on the folded-over tongue. Punch them through both the tongue and top layers. Mark an even number of thong holes around the top ½″ from the edge and spaced about 1½″ apart. Punch these holes and put in tie thongs; start by going down through the tongue, and weave the thong in and out. Tie the ends in a square knot.

7. *Bottom sole:* Following directions on page 52, cut out and glue on a rubber or leather bottom sole.

8. *Sponge insole* (optional): Outline the foot on sponge, cut it out, and slip the insole into the moccasin.

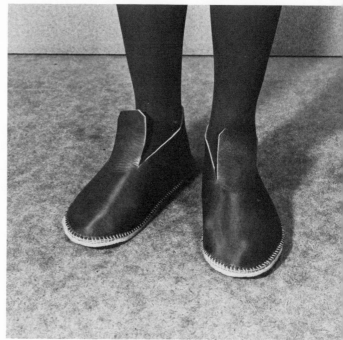

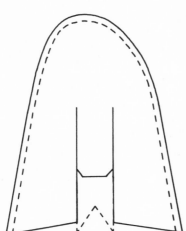

These moccasins are made with the Shoshone pattern, with these changes.

1. Extend the tongue lines 1″ toward the toe end.

2. Shorten the tongue, cutting off the fork; the tongue in the photo extends back 2½″ from the new ends of the slits. Cut small triangles off the corners to shape the tongue.

3. Add ⅜″ to the outer, curved edge of the top-piece pattern (but do not add to the heel seam edges).

Cut both top and sole of 4-to-5- or 5-to-6-ounce retanned cowhide. Mark hole placement and punch sewing holes in both top and sole (step 2). Whipstitch the top to the sole (step 4), using a harness needle instead of a glover's needle. Sew the back seam (step 5). Omit the tie thong (but thong holes can be punched and retanned tie thongs added if desired).

KIOWA

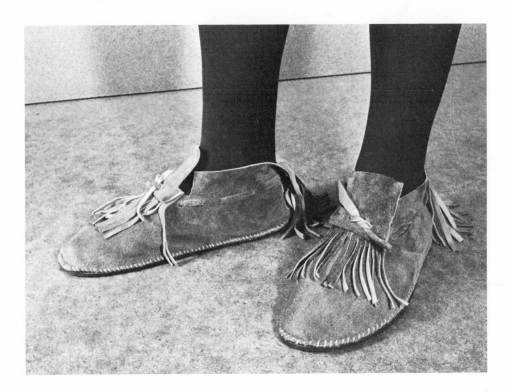

Materials: Retanned cowhide for soles, soft leather for tops, thread, about 5 feet of thong, rubber or leather and glue for bottom soles, sponge (optional)

Tools: Cutter, stitchmarker (optional), #oo punch, glover's needle, stapler (optional), larger punch for thong holes (optional)

THE PATTERN

1. Make the sole and top-piece patterns the same as the Shoshone patterns (page 81), through step 6.

2. Measure ¾″ out from the heel on the heel-toe line and draw a line perpendicular to the heel-toe line at that point.

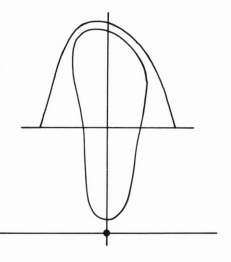

3. Measure from the floor up the back of your foot to where you want the moccasin to reach—probably between 3″ and 4″. Add 1″ and mark points on the line you drew in step 2 that distance from the heel-toe line on each side.

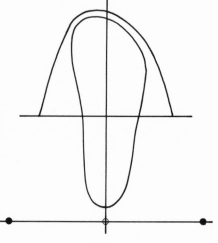

4. Continue the curve to connect the front and back. The ends of the curve meet the heel line at the points you marked in step 3.

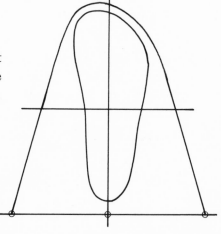

5. Extend the back 2″ for the fringe.

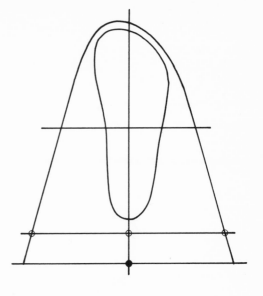

6. Measure the length of the foot outline on the heel-toe line and mark a point 1″ closer than halfway to the toe end. Erase the heel-toe line from the toe end to this point.

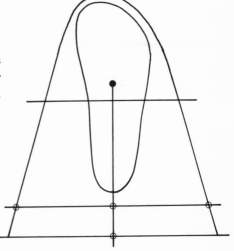

7. Draw a line 2″ long, centered on the heel-toe line and perpendicular to it, at the point you marked in step 6.

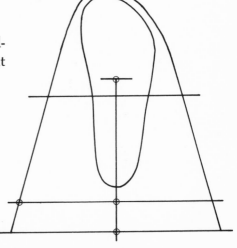

8. Cut out the paper pattern. Cut along the center line and the 2″ line you drew in step 7.

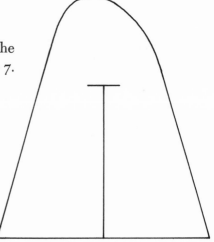

9. Make a pattern for the tongue—a rectangular piece 2″ wide and 7″ long. Cut out the paper pattern.

CONSTRUCTION

1. Using the sole pattern, cut one right and one left of the retanned cowhide. Cut a right and a left top piece and two tongue pieces of the soft leather. On the top piece, cut along the center line and the 2″ line.

2. Mark placement of sewing holes on the sole piece ⅛″ from the edge. Use a stitchmarker or ruler; if you use a ruler, make the marks ³⁄₁₆″ apart. Punch #00 holes at the marked points.

3. Decorate the tops as desired. If you are going to decorate the tongue, put the decorations on the outside of the leather on 1½″ of one end of the piece, because most of the tongue will be fringed (see photo of finished moccasins).

4. Whipstitch the top piece to the sole piece: Place the inside of the top piece on the smooth side of the sole piece (the top-grain side of the sole is placed so that it will be next to the foot; the bottom sole will be glued to the rough side of the leather). Start sewing at the toe, whipstitch around to the heel, and then start again at the toe and sew the other side. Use one sole hole per stitch.

5. Try on the moccasin and hold the heel edges together to see where the heel seam should be; staple them together or mark with a pencil. Starting at the bottom, sew up the heel seam with the right sides out, leaving the top inch unsewn to allow the fringe to flop over the heel.

6. Fold the tongue in half, right sides together. Place the fold on the 2″ tongue cut of the top piece, with the ends of the tongue down toward the toe end. Whipstitch the folded tongue onto the top piece.

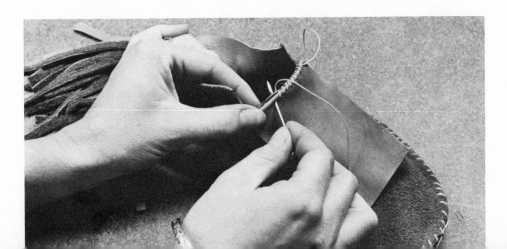

7. Cut the fringe on the bottom part of the tongue and in the back (see photo of finished moccasins); make fringes ⅛″ to ³⁄₁₆″ wide. It's easier to cut fringe with shears than with a razor cutter. If you only have a cutter, put in a new blade for the fringe cutting. Cut slowly, moving the leather, not the cutter, as explained on page 27. If you're a perfectionist, you can measure the fringe cuts and mark them lightly with a pencil before cutting. You'll probably have to trim off some of the lower back fringe so you won't trip on it.

8. Mark the position of thong holes: Fold 2½″ of the top part of the tongue up away from the toe, so that the outside of the leather is showing. Mark and punch two thong holes on the folded-over tongue. You will be punching through four layers—three of tongue and one of top. Mark an even number of thong holes around the top 1″ from the edge and spaced about 1″ apart.

Punch these holes and put in tie thongs; start by going down through the tongue and weave the thong in and out. Tie the ends in a square knot.

92

9. *Bottom sole:* Following the directions on page 52, cut out and glue on a rubber or leather bottom sole.

10. *Sponge insole* (optional): Outline the foot on sponge, cut it out, and slip the insole into the moccasin.

BEADED, UNFRINGED VARIATION

The beaded moccasins in the photo were made by Alice Kinzel of the Sioux Indian Reservation at Lame Deer, Montana. To make a pair like them, use the Kiowa directions, but omit the fringe at the heel and on the tongue. Make the tongue about one-third as long as for Kiowa and sew it onto the top at one end rather than folded in half. Punch two tie thong holes in the top near the front corners.

OSAGE

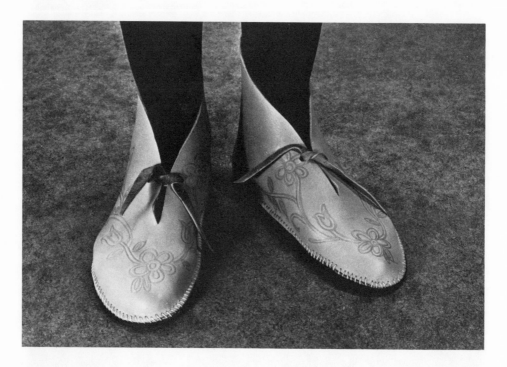

Materials: Retanned cowhide for soles, soft leather for tops, thread, about 2 feet of thong, rubber or leather and glue for bottom soles, sponge (optional)

Tools: Cutter, stitchmarker (optional), #00 punch, glover's needle, larger punch for thong holes (optional)

THE PATTERN

1. *Sole:* Draw a foot outline. Draw a line ¼″ out from the outline all the way around and cut the pattern out.

2. *Top:* Draw another foot outline. Draw a heel-toe line in the middle of the foot (see page 25).

3. Mark a point 2″ out from the heel on the heel-toe line and draw a line there perpendicular to the heel-toe line.

4. Measure up the back of your foot to decide how high you want the back of the moccasin to reach. Mine is about 6″ high—don't go more than 2″ off that or you might have problems.

On each side, measure this distance from the heel-toe line along the heel line you drew in step 3 and mark points.

5. Draw a line ¼″ out from the toes, beginning where the toes join the foot on each side. With straight lines, connect the ends of the curve to the points you marked in step 4.

6. Measure all the way around your foot outline (the perimeter) and divide the measurement in half. Write down the halved measurement.

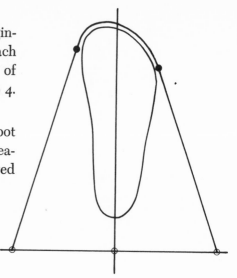

7. Starting at the toe, measure off this distance (half of the foot perimeter) along the lines you drew in step 5, and mark the point on each side. Connect these points to the point where the heel-toe line meets the heel line, as shown.

8. Mark a point about 4″ in from the toe curve on the heel-toe line—you will be cutting from the back of the pattern to this point for the foot opening.

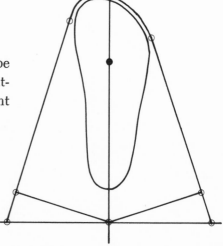

9. Cut out the paper pattern and cut the slit for the foot opening.

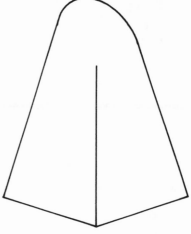

CONSTRUCTION

1. Using the sole pattern, cut one right and one left of the retanned cowhide. Cut a right and a left top piece of the soft leather. Cut the slits for the foot openings.

2. Mark placement of sewing holes on the sole piece ⅛″ from the edge. Use a stitchmarker or a ruler; if you use a ruler, make the marks ³⁄₁₆″ apart. Punch #00 holes at the marked points.

3. Decorate the tops as desired. If you are not going to turn down a cuff, put all decorations on the outside of the leather; if you are going to turn down a cuff and you want to decorate the cuff area, put the decorations on the inside of the leather so that they will show when the cuff is turned down.

4. Whipstitch the top piece to the sole piece: Place the inside of the top piece on the smooth side of the sole piece (the top-grain side of the sole is placed so that it will be next to the foot; the bottom sole will be glued to the rough side of the leather). Start sewing at the toe, and whipstitch around to the heel, then start again at the toe and sew the other side. Use one sole hole per stitch. Keep checking as you go to see that you're not pulling things out of shape, and that you have enough top piece to get all the way to the heel. If you don't have quite enough, you can stretch the top piece very slightly with each stitch to make it fit.

5. Try on the moccasin and hold the heel edges together to check the fit. Trim off at the heel edges if necessary, leaving ⅛″ for the seam. Starting at the bottom, sew up the back seam, right sides out.

6. Punch two holes for the thong. Put the holes close to the foot to make the moccasin fit. You can turn down the back to make a cuff, if you want, or leave it up.

7. *Bottom sole:* Following the directions on page 52, cut out and glue on a rubber or leather bottom sole.

8. *Sponge insole* (optional): Outline the foot on sponge, cut it out, and slip the insole into the moccasin.

SHEARLING VARIATION

The moccasins in the photograph are made of shearling suede with the Osage pattern. The pattern was not adjusted to allow for the thickness of the shearling, since this pattern does not fit tightly around the ankle. Other patterns might need to be changed for use with shearling.

FLATHEAD

Materials: Soft leather, thread, about 6 feet of thong, sponge (optional), leather and glue for bottom soles (optional)

Tools: Cutter, stapler, glover's needle, punch for thong holes

THE PATTERN

1. Make a foot-piece pattern following the instructions for Winnebago (page 62), steps 1–8.

2. Draw a line for the foot opening: Measure on your foot from the tip of your longest toe to where the leg bend starts. This measurement does not have to be exact; mine is 6″. Mark a point on the heel-toe line this distance from the toe end of the pattern. Draw a line 2″ long, centered on the heel-toe line and perpendicular to it, at the point you just marked. Erase the portion of the heel-toe line between this 2″ line and the toe end.

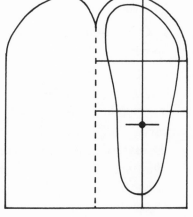

99

3. Cut the pattern along the foot opening line and the 2″ line, as shown.

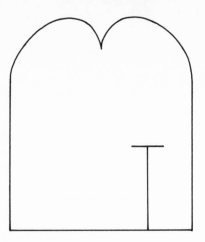

4. *Tongue:* Make a pattern that is a rectangle 3½″ wide and 6″ long. Cut out the tongue pattern.

5. *Leg piece:* Make a rectangular pattern 6″ high and as long as the distance around the foot outline (the perimeter). Cut out the leg-piece pattern.

CONSTRUCTION

1. Cut a right and a left of the foot piece and make the T-shaped foot-opening cuts. Cut two tongues and two leg pieces.

2. Fold the foot piece in half along the fold line of the pattern, right sides out. Staple the seam (⅛″ from the edge) from the fold to the end of the curve. Put your foot in the foot piece with the T-shaped cut on the top and the stapled edge on the outside of the foot. If the piece is too loose, put in more staples to make it fit snugly. Take off the moccasin and trim the curve if necessary to ⅛″ outside the line of staples. Pull out the staples. Decorate the pieces as desired.

3. Fold the foot piece in half along the fold line again, right sides *in*. Whipstitch from the fold to the end of the curve.

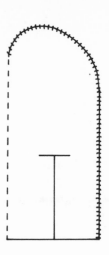

4. Turn the moccasin right side out, put your foot in, and hold the heel edges together to check the fit. Trim off at the heel if necessary, leaving ⅛″ for the seam. Turn the moccasin wrong side out again and sew the heel seam: Fold the moccasin so that the stitching meets the fold line and the top edges of the foot piece match, forming a vertical seam down the back. Starting at the top, whipstitch these edges together to within ¾″ of the bottom. Notice that the seam you made in step 3 does not run along the floor line, but slants up to meet the heel seam about halfway up.

5. Now refold the moccasin so that a short horizontal seam is formed (see photograph) and whipstitch across. (Completed heel seam is shown on page 102).

6. Attach the tongue: Center 3½″ edge of the tongue on the 2″ cut of the foot piece, right sides together, and whipstitch the edges together.

7. Attach the leg piece: Center the long edge of the leg piece on the top edge of the foot piece, right sides together. Begin sewing (whipstitch) at the middle of the back and sew to one side, then start at the back again and sew to the other side.

8. Turn the moccasin right side out and try it on. Turn the tongue up toward the leg and tuck in the extra on the sides. Wrap the leg piece around the leg, allowing 2″ or 3″ of overlap, and mark for trimming if there is excess. Take off the moccasin and trim the leg piece if necessary; you can also round the corners of the leg piece if desired.

9. Punch holes for tie thongs, one on each side, near the corners where the tongue is sewn on, and thread thongs in one hole and out the other. The long thongs wrap around as many times as you want.

10. *Sponge insole* (optional): Outline the foot on sponge, cut it out, and slip the insole into the moccasin.

11. *Bottom sole* (optional): Following the directions on page 52, cut out and glue on a leather bottom sole (this moccasin is too soft for a rubber sole).

LOW, FRINGED VARIATION

The fringed moccasins in the photo were made by Louise McDonald of the Flathead Indian Reservation at St. Ignatius, Montana. The leather is Indian-tanned deerskin.

To make a pair like these, use the Flathead directions. Make the leg piece much lower (about 2½″) and only long enough for the actual sewing distance—no overlap. Sew it on and turn it down like a cuff. Fringe the lower edge. The tongue should also be much shorter—about 2″ long. Make a few fringing cuts in the top of the tongue if desired. Punch two thong holes, one in each end of the fringed cuff, so the thong will tie over the tongue.

Northwest Type
Moccasin

MUKLUK

Materials: Plywood for sole mold; retanned cowhide for soles, soft leather for tops, thread, 6 to 8 feet of ⅝" to ¾" thong (the larger amount is for very high moccasins), 4 feet of ¼" thong, sponge (optional), rubber or leather and glue for bottom soles (optional)

Tools: Saw, drill, clamp, sandpaper for mold; cutter, stitchmarker (optional), #00 punch, glover's needle, larger punch for thong holes (optional)

The pattern and construction are not separate steps here, because the Mukluk vamp must be sewed to the sole before the leg-and-heel-piece pattern is made. For this reason, you won't be able to take the complete pattern along when you go to buy the leather. You can draw the vamp pattern, buy leather for vamp and sole, and construct the moccasins through step 7, then make the leg-and-heel-piece pattern and make a second trip to buy the rest of the leather. Or you can make a temporary leg-and-heel-piece pattern, estimating the measurements, and buy all the leather at once. (Buy a little bit more leather than you think you'll need, to make sure you'll have enough.)

THE PATTERN AND CONSTRUCTION

1. Make a pair of molded soles and punch sewing holes in them, following the directions on pages 29–33.

2. *Vamp:* Draw a foot outline. Draw a heel-toe line in the middle of the foot (see page 25).

3. Find the halfway point between heel and toe on the foot outline; mark the point and draw a line perpendicular to the heel-toe line at that point.

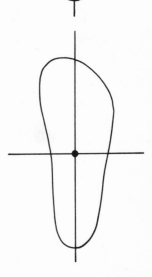

4. Place the molded sole on the foot outline and put your foot in it. Measure across the arch from sole edge to sole edge at the midline (see page 24). Center the measurement on the midline.

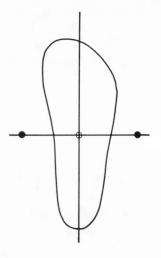

5. Draw a curve that follows the foot outline around the toes and then straightens out down to the points you marked in step 4, as shown.

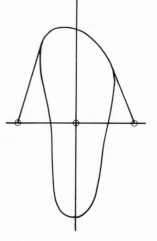

6. Measure 1″ in from the heel on the heel-toe line and draw straight lines connecting the ends of the lines you drew in step 5 to that point. This completes the vamp pattern. Cut it out, and cut a left and a right of leather. Decorate as you wish.

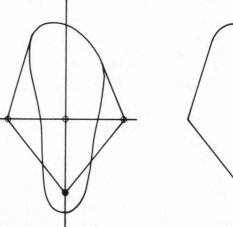

7. Whipstitch the vamp to the sole, right sides out. Start at the toe and sew around one side, then start again at the toe and sew around the other side, using one sole hole per stitch. Keep checking the alignment of the vamp as you sew so you don't stretch it out of shape.

8. *Leg and heel piece:* Put your foot in the molded sole. At the heel, measure up from the top of the sole to determine how high you want the moccasins to reach. Mine are 10″ high; they can be high enough to reach to just below the knee (see variation below)—in fact high ones will stay up better, because of the curve of the calf. Add 1″ to the measurement and, on a piece of pattern paper, draw a straight line that length. Then draw lines perpendicular to it at each end, as shown.

9. Measure around the heel of the molded sole, from the point where the vamp stops to the point where it starts on the other side. Center and mark this distance on the lower line you drew in step 8.

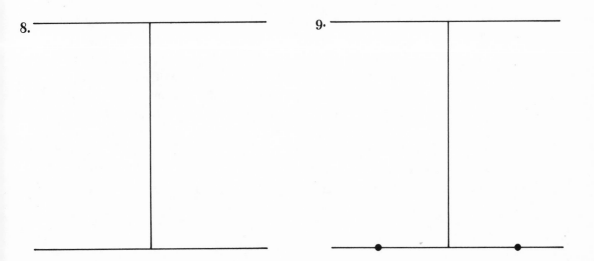

10. Now mark points 2″ farther out on each side and draw vertical lines through them, connecting the upper and lower lines (see page 108).

11. Measure one straight side of the vamp piece, from where it is sewn to the sole to the pointed end. Make lines this length angling up to the lines you drew in step 10, beginning your measurements at the heel points you marked in step 9. This completes the leg-and-heel-piece pattern.

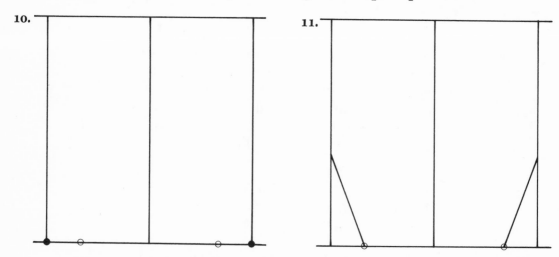

12. Cut out the pattern. Check the fit by wrapping it around your leg to make sure that the piece is big enough. The straight sides (above the slanted edges) of the pattern meet at the front of your leg; the bottom (between the slanted edges) is the heel piece, which will attach to the back of the molded sole. The pattern should meet at the front, allowing for a ⅛″ seam. If the pattern isn't big enough, measure on your leg to see how much more is needed. Draw around the pattern on another piece of paper. Add half of the extra inches needed to each side at the front seam edges. Redraw the vamp seam edge if necessary, so that it still measures the same length. Cut out the new wider pattern and try it on to see if it is now big enough.

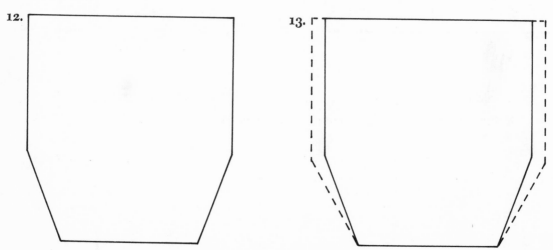

13. Cut out two leg and heel pieces from leather. Cut four tie strips ⅝″ to ¾″ wide and 18″ to 24″ long (the longer tie strips are for higher moccasins). Cut slanted ends on the tie strips. Cut ¼″ thongs for the drawstrings at the top of the moccasins—two thongs, each about 2 feet long.

14. Whipstitch the heel piece to the sole, right sides out. Start at the back of the heel and sew around one side, then start again at the heel and sew around the other side, using one sole hole per stitch. Stretch the heel piece a bit if necessary to make it meet the vamp piece—and trim it a bit if it overlaps, allowing ⅛″ for the seam between vamp and leg and heel piece.

When you have sewed about 2″ from the heel on one side, include a tie strip in the seam. Place the tie strip, slanted to the rear, on top of the heel piece, catch it in the seam, and then continue the seam. Include the second tie strip in the seam on the other side. (If you forget to include the tie strips in the seam, sew them on separately after finishing the seam.)

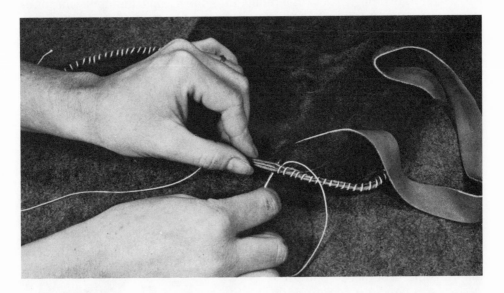

15. Sew the slanted part of the leg piece to the vamp, right sides out; sew first one side, then the other, meeting at the point. Even with careful pattern-making, the edges may not meet evenly at the point, but don't worry; the front edges can be trimmed a little if necessary to make the point come out right. Sew on up the front seam (right sides out) to the top of the leg piece.

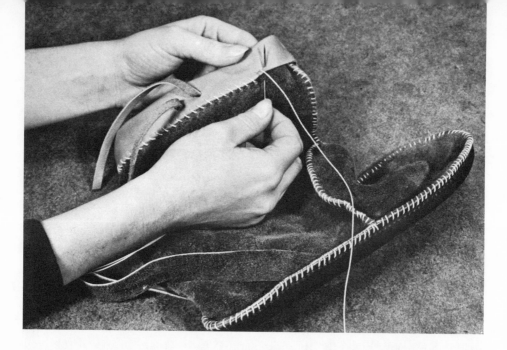

16. Punch two holes in the top of the leg piece for the thong to emerge from; place the holes 1″ apart and ½″ from the edge, on the outside of the leg piece. Turn 1″ of the top of the leg piece down to the outside to make a casing for the thong. Tuck the thong into the casing and pull the ends through the holes. Then whipstitch the cuff in place.

When the moccasins are worn, the tie strips cross in the back and wrap around the leg as many times as you like, tying where you want them to.

17. *Sponge insole* (optional): Outline the foot on sponge, cut it out, and slip the insole into the moccasin.

18. *Bottom sole* (optional): Following the directions on page 52, cut out and glue on a rubber or leather bottom sole.

HIGH VARIATION

For a knee-high Mukluk, draw the leg-and-heel-piece pattern about 17″ high, or the measurement up to just below your kneecap plus 1″.

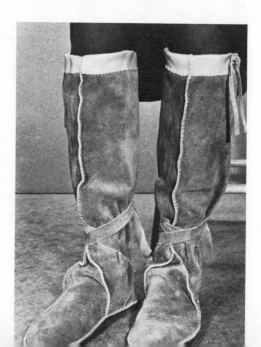

Southwest Type Moccasins

NAVAJO

Materials: Plywood for sole mold; retanned leather for soles, tracing paper, tape for joining pattern pieces, soft leather for tops, thread, about 18″ of ¼″ thong, two conchas (optional—a concha is a decorative metal button with holes in it for thongs), sponge (optional), rubber or leather and glue for bottom soles (optional)

Tools: Saw, drill, clamp, sandpaper for mold; cutter, #00 punch, glover's needle, larger punch for thong holes (optional)

First make a pair of molded soles and punch sewing holes in them, following the directions on pages 29–33.

following the directions on pages 29–33.

THE PATTERN

1. Draw a foot outline. Draw a heel-toe line in the middle of the foot (see page 25).

2. Draw a curved line ¼″ out from the toes, beginning where the toes join the foot on each side.

3. Find the halfway point between heel and toe on the foot outline; mark the point and draw a line perpendicular to the heel-toe line at that point.

Place the molded sole on the foot outline and put your foot in it. Measure across the arch from sole edge to sole edge at the midline (see page 24). Add ¼″, and center the resulting measurement on the midline.

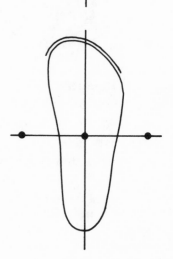

4. Draw straight lines connecting the points you made in step 3 with the ends of the toe curve, as shown.

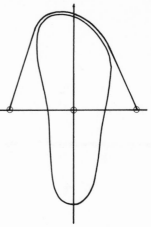

5. Using tracing paper, trace the printed pattern on page 114, allowing space for your toe pattern where indicated. Trace the other part of the pattern (page 115), cut out the two pieces, and tape them together at the dotted lines. Place your toe pattern on the tracing, matching the X's with the X's on the traced pattern. Make sure that you have placed the inside-of-foot side of your toe pattern on the inside-of-foot side of the traced pattern. Draw around the toe pattern and cut out the toe part, making one complete pattern piece.

Inside of foot

6. Check the pattern to make sure that it is long enough to go around the sole. Measure the distance around the sole's top edge, and then measure the pattern from the outside-of-foot X, around the toe pattern, past the inside-of-foot X, and around the bottom edge of the leg piece curve to the vertical line ending the curve. Compare the measurements. If the toe-and-leg-piece measurement is greater than the sole measurement, that's fine—the piece can be trimmed later. But if the toe-and-leg-piece measurement is smaller than the sole measurement, you'll have to add to the leg-piece curve. Place the pattern on another piece of paper and draw around it, adding the necessary length at the end of the curve, as indicated on the diagram.

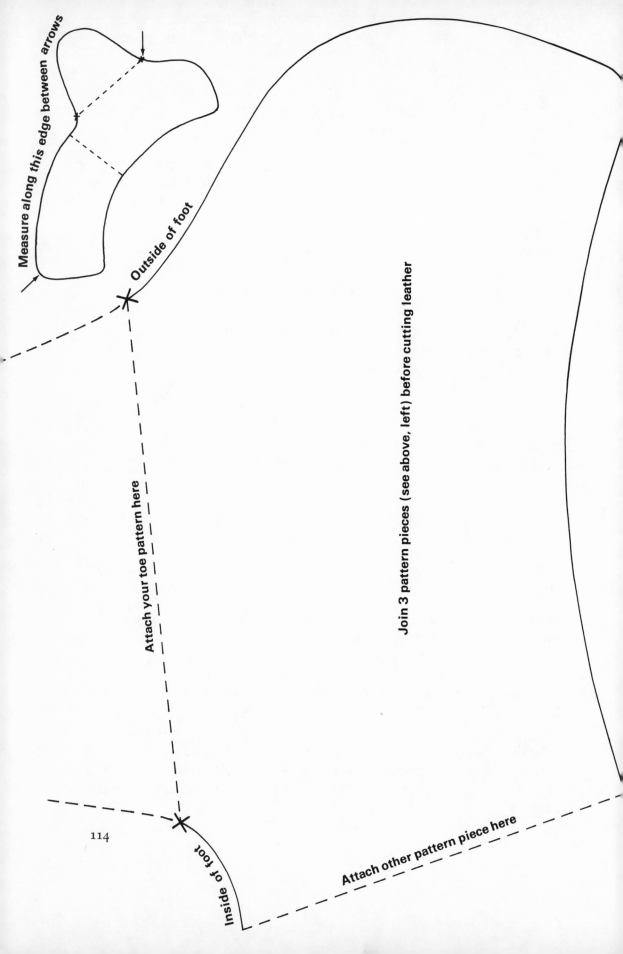

Measure along this edge between arrows

Outside of foot

Attach your toe pattern here

Inside of foot

Join 3 pattern pieces (see above, left) before cutting leather

Attach other pattern piece here

114

Add length here if needed (step 6)

Join 3 pattern pieces (see above, left) before cutting leather

Attach other pattern piece here

115

CONSTRUCTION

1. Cut out one right and one left of the soft leather, and decorate as desired.

2. Align the toe piece on the molded sole. Use a glover's needle to make *just one* whipstitch through top and bottom at the tip of the toe, and tie the thread in a knot. Make several more of these single stitches on each side of the toe piece so that you can check the fit. Put your foot in the moccasin. If the toe seems too loose, mark and trim off the excess, leaving ⅛″ for the seam.

3. Take out the basting stitches you made in step 2. Now whipstitch the top onto the sole, using one sole hole per stitch. Start at the toe and sew toward the inside of the foot and around the heel until you have reached the ankle on the *outside* of the foot. Then sew from the toe around the outside of the foot. Stop an inch or so before the end and try on the moccasin. Pull the flap down snug around the foot and mark the leather with a pencil for trimming, if necessary. Trim the outside flap and finish the seam, making the outside piece overlap the one that comes around the heel from the inside. Try on the moccasin, mark the inside flap for trimming, and trim it if necessary.

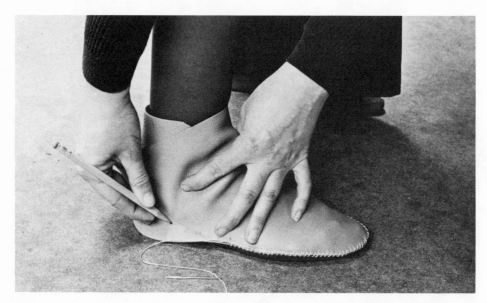

4. Try on the moccasin once more, to see where you want the two thong holes. Mine are 2″ up from the edge of the sole. Make one 1″ from the edge of the flap, the other ½″ in from there. Punch the holes through the two layers of leather and put in the tie thong. Add a concha, if desired, threading the thongs through the concha holes. Tie the thong ends together in a single knot and cut off excess thong, leaving about 1″ on the ends after the knot is tied.

5. *Sponge insole* (optional): Outline the foot on sponge, cut it out, and slip the insole into the moccasin.

6. *Bottom sole* (optional): Following the directions on page 52, cut out and glue on a rubber or leather bottom sole.

APACHE

Materials: Plywood for sole mold; retanned cowhide for soles, tracing paper, tape for joining pattern pieces, soft leather for tops, thread, about

4 feet of thong, sponge (optional), rubber or leather and glue for bottom soles (optional)

Tools: Saw, drill, clamp, sandpaper for mold; cutter, stitchmarker (optional), #00 punch, glover's needle, larger punch for thong holes (optional)

First make a pair of molded soles and punch sewing holes in them, following the directions on pages 29–33.

THE PATTERN

1. *Vamp:* Draw a foot outline. Draw a heel-toe line in the middle of the foot (see page 25).

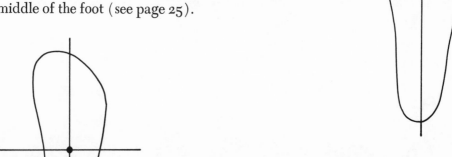

2. Find the halfway point between heel and toe on the foot outline; mark the point and draw a line perpendicular to the heel-toe line at that point. Put your foot on the foot outline and measure over the arch to the floor at the point you just marked (see page 23). Write down the measurement.

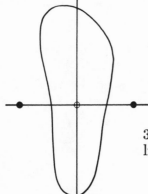

3. Center the measurement from step 2 on the midline.

4. Find the halfway point between the midline and the toe of the foot outline; mark the point and draw a line perpendicular to the heel-toe line at that point. Put your foot on the foot outline and measure over the arch to the floor at the new point. Write down the measurement.

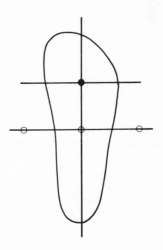

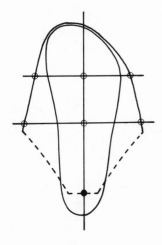

5. Center the new measurement from step 4 on the new line you drew in step 4.

6. Draw a curve through the points you drew in steps 3 and 5 and a point $\frac{1}{16}''$ out from the foot outline at the toe, as shown. You want the curve snug around the toes, to hold the moccasin on. Extend the lines $\frac{1}{2}''$ beyond the midline, as shown.

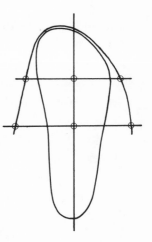

7. Draw a shape for the tongue. This can be left big and unshaped if you like, and trimmed after everything is sewn together. I make mine about 1″ short of the heel in the foot outline, and about 1½″ wide at the end, cut straight across, as shown in the diagram.

119

8. Cut out the vamp pattern.

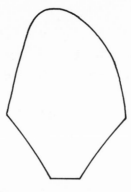

9. *Back piece:* Measure the length of the molded sole to find the half-way point between heel and toe. With a measuring tape, measure around the back of the molded sole to the halfway point on each side. Add 1″ to the measurement (to provide an overlap of vamp and back).

10. There is a printed pattern for the back piece on page 121. Using tracing paper, trace it twice; then cut out the tracings and lay them together as shown, matching the dotted lines. Measure the pattern's lower edge and compare this with the back measurement from step 9. If it is the same, tape the two pattern-piece halves together as they are.

If the back pattern is too short, place the pieces on another piece of paper and spread the dotted line edges apart evenly to lengthen the pattern the correct amount, as indicated on the diagram. Draw around the pattern and cut it out.

If the back pattern is too long, overlap the dotted line edges evenly to shorten it the correct amount. Tape the pieces together.

To check the height of the back piece, put your foot in the molded sole and measure 4″ from the sole edge up the back of your ankle. If this is not high enough for you, you can make the pattern higher by extending the sides of the pattern at the top and drawing a parallel curve.

CONSTRUCTION

1. Cut two back pieces and a left and a right vamp piece. Decorate as desired.

2. Whipstitch the vamp to the sole, right sides out, using one sole hole per stitch. Start at the toe and sew around one side, then start at the toe again

**Trace pattern twice and join pieces as shown below
before cutting leather**

Check measurement along this edge

To make higher, add at top

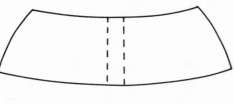

To widen, spread pieces apart

121

To make narrower, overlap pieces

and sew around the other side. The vamp might not reach to the same point on both sides of the moccasin, but this doesn't matter, since it will be covered by the back piece.

3. Whipstitch the back piece to the sole, right sides out, using one sole hole per stitch. Start at the heel and sew around one side, then start at the heel again and sew around the other side, making the back piece overlap the vamp on each side. It's a good idea to stretch the back piece just a little as you sew around the heel, to make the heel fit snugly.

Put on the moccasin and mark the tongue and the corners that fold over it for trimming; trim them if necessary.

4. Punch an even number of holes in the back piece, spaced about 1″ apart and 1½″ from the top edge. Put in the thong, starting at one side and weaving the thong in and out. Turn down about 1″ of the top to form a cuff.

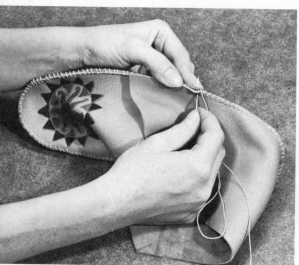 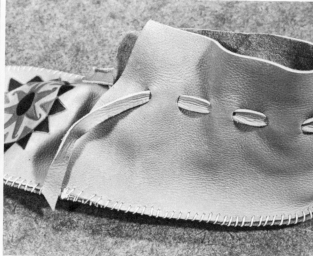

5. *Sponge insole* (optional): Outline the foot on sponge, cut it out, and slip the insole into the moccasin.

6. *Bottom sole* (optional): Following the directions on page 52, cut out and glue on a rubber or leather bottom sole.

122

LOW RETANNED VARIATION

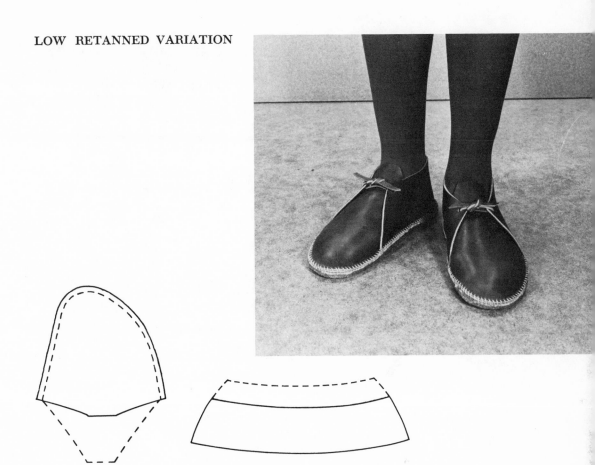

To make these flat-soled retanned cowhide moccasins, follow the Shoshone directions to make a sole pattern, cut out the soles, mark hole placement, and punch holes (see pages 81 and 84). Make vamp and back-piece patterns as for Apache, with these changes:

1. Add ⅜″ to the curved toe edge of the vamp (but not to the tongue edges).

2. Make the tongue 2″ shorter.

3. Lower the top edge of the back piece 1½″ by drawing a parallel curve.

Cut the vamp and back pieces from 4-to-5- or 5-to-6-ounce retanned cowhide. Mark and punch sewing holes in the sewing edges, the same as for the sole. Follow the Apache construction directions, but use a harness needle instead of a glover's needle. Punch two thong holes, one in each corner of the back piece, and put in about 1 foot of retanned thong. Tie the ends in a square knot. A bottom sole is essential to protect the stitching.

FRINGED VARIATION

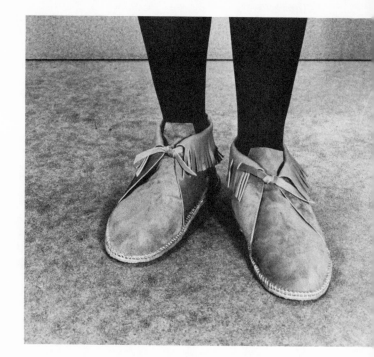

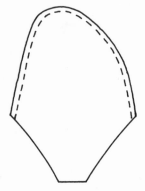

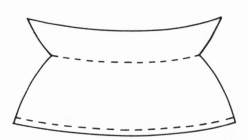

To make these fringed, flat-soled moccasins, follow the Shoshone directions to make a sole pattern, cut out the soles, mark hole placement, and punch holes (see pages 81 and 84). Make vamp and back-piece patterns as for Apache, with these changes:

1. Add ⅜″ to the curved toe edge of the vamp (but not to the tongue edges).

2. Add ⅜″ to the lower edge of the back piece.

3. Add 1½″ to the upper edge of the back piece to make a cuff, by drawing a parallel curve as shown in the diagram.

Construct the moccasins following the Apache directions. Turn down the cuff and fringe it. A bottom sole is essential to protect the stitching.

Glossary

Arch: The middle section of the foot—the part that forms an arching upward curve between toes and heel.

Bottom sole: A second layer of leather or rubber glued to the bottom (floor) side of the moccasin sole.

Heel-toe line: A straight line drawn lengthwise, between heel and toe, in the middle of the foot outline.

Inside of foot: The side of the foot next to the other foot; the big-toe side.

Insole: A foot-shaped piece of material that slips inside the moccasin; in this book, the material is always sponge rubber.

Midline: A straight line drawn across the foot outline at right angles (perpendicular) to the heel-toe line, at the halfway point between heel and toe.

Outside of foot: The side of the foot away from the other foot; the little-toe side.

Parallel lines: Lines extending in the same direction, the same distance apart at every point.

Perimeter: The distance around the foot outline.

Perpendicular: A line at right angles to another line.

Tongue: A piece of a moccasin that extends from the midsection of the foot toward the leg, often tucking under overlaps. The tongue might be a short curved shape on the end of the vamp, or it might be a long, narrow strip sewn to the moccasin top.

Vamp: A piece of a moccasin that covers the top of the foot, including the toes and part or all of the arch.

Suppliers

All the suppliers listed below sell by mail order.

Berman Leathercraft
147 South Street
Boston, Mass. 02111

Century Leather Co., Inc.
110 Beach Street
Boston, Mass. 02111

Cleveland Leather Co.
2824 Lorain Avenue
Cleveland, Ohio 44113

Colo-Craft
1310 S. Broadway
Denver, Colo. 80210

The Dead Cow
1040 River Street
Santa Cruz, Calif. 95060

D'Narb Ltd.
100 Myrtle Avenue
Havertown, Pa. 19083

Double D Leather Co.
6212 D Madison Pike
Huntsville, Ala. 35806

Drake Leather Co., Inc.
3500 W. Beverly Blvd.
Montebello, Calif. 90640

Funk and Rose
212 S. 15th Avenue
Minneapolis, Minn. 55404

Leather
19 E. Woodside Avenue
Ardmore, Pa. 19003

Leathercrafters' Supply Co.
25 Great Jones Street
New York, N.Y. 10012

Leather Etc.
2033 University Avenue
Berkeley, Calif. 94704

Leather Unlimited Co.
P. O. Box 23002
Milwaukee, Wis. 53223

The Leather Works
628 Emerson Street
Palo Alto, Calif. 94301

Leon Leather Co., Inc.
1738 E. 2nd Street
Scotch Plains, N.J. 07076

Mac Leather Co.
424 Broome Street
New York, N.Y. 10013

MacPherson Brothers
200 S. Los Angeles Street
Los Angeles, Calif. 90033
and
1337 5th Avenue
San Diego, Calif. 92101
and
730 Polk Street
San Francisco, Calif. 94109
and
1209 2nd Avenue
Seattle, Wash. 98101

Natural Leather
203 Bleecker Street
New York, N.Y. 10012

New Haven Leather Co.,
Inc.
254 State Street
New Haven, Conn. 06510
(mail order in Conn. area
only)

Oregon Leather Co.
110 N.W. 2nd Avenue
Portland, Ore. 97209

J. G. Read & Bros. Co., Inc.
101 21st Street, Box 469
Ogden, Utah 84402

Richmond Leather Co.
1839 W. Broad Street
Richmond, Va. 23220

Southwestern Leather &
Shoe Findings Co.
27 N. 3rd Avenue, Box 3555
Phoenix, Ariz. 85030

S-T Leather Co.
329-33 E. Long Street
Columbus, Ohio 43215
and
4018 Olive Street
St. Louis, Mo. 63108

Tandy Leather Co.
many stores (look in the
phone book)

Worth Leather Co.
151 Allen Blvd.
Farmingdale, N.Y. 11735

Suggestions for Further Reading

INDIAN CRAFTS IN GENERAL

The Complete How-To Book of Indiancraft. W. Ben Hunt. New York: Collier
  Books, 1973.
  Includes information on Indian tanning and good design ideas.
Crafts for North American Indian Arts. Mary Lou Stribling. New York: Crown
  Publishers, 1975.
  Contains valuable information on beadwork.
Crafts of the North America Indians, a Craftsman's Manual. Richard C.
  Schneider. New York: Van Nostrand Reinhold Co., 1972.
  Includes complete information on Indian tanning and useful material on bead-
  work.

BEADWORK

American Indian Beadwork. W. Ben Hunt and J. F. "Buck" Burshears. New York:
  Collier Books, 1951.
  Also a useful source for design ideas.
How to Do Beadwork. Mary White. New York: Dover Publications, 1972 (re-
  print of 1904 edition).
Step by Step Beadcraft. Judith Glassman. New York: Golden Press, 1974.

DESIGN IDEAS

American Indian Design and Decoration. Leroy H. Appleton. New York: Dover
  Publications, 1971 (reprint of 1951 edition).
Authentic Indian Designs. Edited by Maria Naylor. New York: Dover Publica-
  tions, 1975.
Decorative Art of the Southwestern Indians. Dorothy Smith Sides. New York:
  Dover Publications, 1946 (reprint of 1932 edition).
Design Motifs of Ancient Mexico. Jorge Encisco. New York: Dover Publications,
  1953 (reprint of 1947 edition).
Hornung's Handbook of Designs and Devices. Clarence P. Hornung. New York:
  Dover Publicatons, 1946 (reprint of 1932 edition).
Pueblo Designs. H. P. Mera. New York: Dover Publications, 1970 (reprint of
  1938 edition).